*James S. Carpentier Lectures*

# SOME PROBLEMS OF PROOF UNDER THE ANGLO-AMERICAN SYSTEM OF LITIGATION

EDMUND MORRIS MORGAN

# SOME PROBLEMS OF PROOF UNDER THE ANGLO-AMERICAN SYSTEM OF LITIGATION

GREENWOOD PRESS, PUBLISHERS
WESTPORT, CONNECTICUT

**Library of Congress Cataloging in Publication Data**

Morgan, Edmund Morris, 1878-1966.
Some problems of proof under the Anglo-American system of litigation.

Reprint of the ed. published by Columbia University Press, New York, in series: James S. Carpentier lectures, 1955.
Includes index.
1. Evidence (Law)--United States. I. Title. II. Series: James S. Carpentier lectures ; 1955.
KF8935.Z9M65 1975 347'.73'6 75-31438
ISBN 0-8371-8517-3



Originally published in 1956 by Columbia University Press, New York

Reprinted with the permission of Columbia University Press

Reprinted in 1975 by Greenwood Press, a division of Williamhouse-Regency Inc.

Library of Congress Catalog Card Number 75-31438

ISBN 0-8371-8517-3

Printed in the United States of America

*To ELSIE*

**JAMES S. CARPENTIER**

**LECTURES**

1904–5 *James Bryce, Viscount Bryce*
Law in Its Relations to History
1907–8 *John Chipman Gray*
The Nature and Sources of the Law
1910–11 *Arthur Lionel Smith*
English Political Writers of the Seventeenth and Eighteenth Centuries and the Development of English Political Theory from Hobbes to Burke
*David Jayne Hill*
The Problem of World Organization As Affected by the Nature of the Modern States
1911–12 *Sir Frederick Pollock*
The Genius of the Common Law
1913–14 *Sir Courtenay Ilbert*
The Mechanics of Law Making
1916–17 *Harold Dexter Hazeltine*
English Legal History
1919–20 *Willard Barbour*
English History with Special Reference to the Development of Rights through Procedure
1923–24 *Sir Paul Vinogradoff*
Some Problems of Jurisprudence
1926–27 *Sir William Searle Holdsworth*
The Historians of Anglo-American Law

| | | |
|---|---|
| 1927–28 | *Benjamin Nathan Cardozo* |
| | The Paradoxes of Legal Science |
| 1940–41 | *Sir Cecil Thomas Carr* |
| | Aspects of Administrative Law |
| 1955 | *Edmund Morris Morgan* |
| | Some Problems of Proof under the Anglo-American System of Litigation |

## FOREWORD

Fifty-three years ago General Horace W. Carpentier of the Class of 1848 established the Carpentier Lecture Fund in honor of his brother, James S. Carpentier. The purpose of the Fund was to make possible a series of lectures which would shed significant and penetrating light on the subject of jurisprudence, which General Carpentier believed to be of preeminent importance to society. In his letter of grant addressed to President Nicholas Murray Butler, General Carpentier expressed the desire that the lecturers be "chosen for pre-eminent fitness and ability" and that "this lectureship will be made so honorable that nobody, however great, or distinguished will willingly choose to decline your invitation."

The roster of Carpentier lecturers begins with James Bryce in 1904 and includes such distinguished men of the law as John Chipman Gray, Sir Frederick Pollock, Sir William Holdsworth, and Benjamin Cardozo. The last lecture before the Second World War was given in 1941 by Sir Cecil Thomas Carr. The onset of the war and the problems of the Law School in meeting the wave of students who came in its wake caused a suspension of the Carpentier lectures, but we were able to resume the series in 1955, when Edmund Morris Morgan agreed to deliver six lectures before the Faculty and students of the Columbia Law School and members of the New York Bar on the topic, "Some Problems of Proof under the Anglo-American System of Litigation." They were given in January and April.

Professor Morgan is eminently qualified to speak with authority. He has been a leading participant in several major projects to improve procedure and evidence, and he has had a distinguished teaching career at Harvard and, since his retirement, at Vanderbilt.

I believe that these lectures that follow will be of particular interest to legal scholars and, in general, to the legal profession because they come from Professor Morgan's unusual understanding of the practical problems of proof under our system of litigation and from an over-all understanding of the subject which I believe is scarcely matched elsewhere in the Bar today. It is a great pleasure to express in these pages the appreciation of the Columbia Law School to Professor Morgan for his contribution to this series of lectures and to commend to our alumni and friends and to the legal profession as a whole the thoughts and ideas which he has given us.

WILLIAM C. WARREN

*Kent Hall*
*January 11, 1956*

# PREFACE

EVEN IN TROUBLOUS TIMES when attention is focused upon international tensions and conflicts, the administration of justice between individual and individual and between individual and the government is of prime importance. The principal agencies for the orderly adjustment of controversies involving legal rights and duties are the courts. And the degree of their efficiency in performing this function depends in large measure, as all lawyers but few laymen realize, upon the rules of procedure, including evidence, which govern their proceedings. It therefore seemed to Dean William C. Warren and the Faculty of Law of Columbia University worth while to have the thirteenth series of the James S. Carpentier Lectures devoted to a consideration of some of the procedural rules which appear to hamper the administration of justice in jury trials.

These lectures were delivered in January and April of 1955. Their objective is to direct the attention of judges and lawyers (1) to the obstructions to adequate preparation for trial created by orthodox rules of pleading and discovery, (2) to the unnecessary confusion caused by conflicts of opinion as to the basis of the doctrine of judicial notice and the potential dangers of confusing it with presumptions, (3) to the needless uncertainty as to the distribution of functions between judge and jury by the use of loose and inaccurate language in dealing with the decisions of questions preliminary to the admissibility of evidence, (4) to the practical impossibility of conveying to the jury an intelligent concept of the consequences of the allocation of the burden of persuasion by the use of the currently accepted instructions, and (5) to the barriers to a rational presentation to the jury of materials of high intrinsic relevancy and persuasive value, erected by the hearsay rule and other exclusionary rules. In preparing the lectures for publication, little attempt has been made to eliminate the repetition which is requisite in oral presentation at various intervals to different audiences.

The views expressed are the result of some years of experience in trial practice and of many years spent in the study of procedure and evidence in connection with my efforts to teach these subjects.

E. M. MORGAN

*Nashville, Tennessee*
*November 11, 1955*

## CONTENTS

# SOME PROBLEMS OF PROOF UNDER THE ANGLO-AMERICAN SYSTEM OF LITIGATION

# RELATION OF PLEADING TO PREPARATION FOR TRIAL

THE THEORY of our adversary system of litigation is that each litigant is most interested and will be most effective in seeking, discovering, and presenting the materials which will reveal the strength of his own case and the weakness of his adversary's case so that the truth will emerge to the impartial tribunal that makes the decision. In any litigated case where the result depends upon the resolution of a dispute as to the facts, there are three reasons why this theory requires that the area of dispute be specifically defined. First, if each party is to assemble the materials to support his own contentions and to defeat those of his adversary, he should not be put to the trouble and expense of securing unusable materials or prevented from discovering whatever may be helpful. Second, the tribunal, if it is to act with intelligence and efficiency, must limit the materials accepted for consideration to those which have appreciable probative value. Third, the question for decision must be framed with such definiteness that the answer will constitute a final determination of the particular controversy. These are self-evident truths to every lawyer who has had experience as an arbitrator in a controversy arising from commercial transactions or a labor contract. And the entire nation has recently had a demonstration in the hearings of the McCarthy-Army controversy of the needless expenditure of time and money, as well as the injustice to participants and strangers, wrought in a proceeding, adversary in form, in which the presiding officer of the tribunal was unable or unwilling to enforce orderly procedure by confining the parties and witnesses to relevant material presented in a seemly manner.

A brief account of the evolution of our system of pleading and proof will reveal the extent to which it has from time to time reflected or failed to reflect the impact of these reasons, and particularly the first two.

This should begin with the early Anglo-Norman procedure as reconstructed by Maitland and should end with the Federal Rules of Civil Procedure. It should include consideration of the Norman Inquest, which developed into the jury, and the methods of framing the questions to be answered, by pleadings or otherwise, as well as the means by which the members of the assize, or jurors, secured pertinent data for their answers. It should note the ever increasing complexities in procedure caused (*a*) by attempts to reshape the common-law forms of action to meet changing conditions, and (*b*) by the creation of too easily abused devices which were no doubt designed to benefit litigants by enabling them to have their entire controversy settled in a single proceeding. And it can scarcely omit consideration of the attempts to simplify the definition and disclosure of the issues for trial by so-called fact pleading under the codes and by notice pleading.

*Maitland's Description* Our available records do not give us an accurate account of the earliest Anglo-Norman procedure for determining the issue between the contestants. The chief difficulty which met the party claiming that he had been wronged was getting the wrongdoer before the tribunal, and much of the early law is concerned with the situations which would excuse a defendant from the obligation to appear. For it was the settled practice not to give a decision against him by default in favor of the complaining party. But once the defendant was brought before the justices, how did they determine the area of dispute, the precise question to be answered? Maitland, drawing upon information gleaned from Glanville, Bracton, and Britton and from Norman sources, paints the following composite picture.[1]

> . . . When the parties stand opposite to each other, it then behooves the plaintiff to state his case by his own mouth or that of his pleader. . . . It is a formal statement bristling with sacramental words, an omission of which would be fatal. . . . In a civil action begun by writ, the plaintiff's count must not depart by a hair's breadth from the writ, or there will be a "variance" of which the defendant will take advantage. On the other hand, the brief statement that the writ contains must be expanded by the count. . . . The count on a Writ of Right will often be an elaborate history. A seisin "as of fee and of right" with a taking

[1] 2 Pollock & Maitland, History of English Law 605 *et. seq.* (2d ed. 1899) (the quoted passages are by Maitland). For much of the material used in this lecture I am indebted to various sparkling writings of Maitland; the incomparable essays of James Bradley Thayer, particularly those in his *Preliminary Treatise on Evidence* (1898); the dull tomes of Holdsworth's *History of English Law:* several volumes of the *Year Books;* Bracton's *Notebook;* the unpublished lectures on Legal History by Professor George E. Woodbine of Yale; and modern commentaries on pleading and procedure in books and articles too numerous to mention. This is not to say that they were consulted specifically in the preparation of this lecture, for most of it is the result of too many years' experience in vain attempts to teach procedure.

of "esplees" will be attributed to some ancestor of the demandant, and then the descent of this right will be traced down a pedigree from which no step may be omitted.

It is not enough that the plaintiff should tell his tale: he must offer to prove its truth. In an Appeal of Felony he offers proof "by his body"; in a Writ of Right he offers proof "by the body of a certain free man of his A.B. by name" who or, whose father, witnessed the seisin that has been alleged; in other cases he produces a suit (*secta*) of witnesses. No one is entitled to an answer if he offers nothing but his bare assertion, his *nude parole*. . . .

. . . . If Allan is bringing an action against William, his count, unless there is a provocation to battle, will end with some such words as these: "And if William will confess this, that will seem fair to Allan; but if he will deny it, wrongfully will he deny it, for Allan has here suit good and sufficient, to wit, Ralph and Roger."

At this point each suitor should step forward and say, "This I saw and heard," and "I am ready to do what the court shall award." And so in the writ of right (in which trial was by battle) the proffered champion will speak thus: "This I saw and heard, or, this my father saw and heard and of this when dying he bade me bear witness—and this I am ready to prove by my body when and where the court shall award."

The suitor did not speak under oath nor did the champion. Each was merely supporting the plaintiff by offering to do what the court should deem necessary. In the case of the suitors, the defendant could call for an examination of each of them under oath. Maitland thinks that in such an event, defendant staked his whole case on the examination, but there are at least one or two recorded cases where defendant was permitted to proceed after the suitors had properly corroborated plaintiff's claim. Of course, if they disclosed that they knew nothing about the facts or if they disagreed or otherwise failed to support the claim, the action was dismissed. If there was no demand for examination of the suitors, as was usually the case, there was no difficulty in determining the issue. The court would treat the action as undefended unless the defendant answered by a flat denial. Originally he had to deny the charge literally, word for word, but by the later practice he could do it in more general terms, ending, "and this he is ready and willing to defend when and where he ought as the court shall consider." In the case of the proffer of battle, the offer was to defend by his own body or that of a specified freeman of his "when and where the court shall consider that defend he ought." The function of the court was to order the kind of trial suited to the issue, and to see that the formalities accompanying it were duly observed. When once the rigid requirements as to plaintiff's statement and defendant's denial had been met, the issue was clear; and when the method by which the party who had the privilege or burden of proof by battle, ordeal, oath, or compugation had been determined, the process and result were clear. There was no problem of persuasion. The answer was controlled by supernatural forces.

*Defendant Allowed Additional Pleas* As early as Bracton's time, the defendant had gained the right to interpose what we should call dilatory defenses, though he must also answer by the unqualified denial. Gradually he acquired also the right to plead specially to the merits even defenses that were merely argumentative denials. Whether this procedure was evolved from the possessory assizes, as Maitland thinks, may be open to debate. But there can be no question that the introduction by the Normans of the inquest, first as an administrative instrument and later as a judicial instrument, for the ascertainment of factual data, had a profound influence.

*Trial by Inquest in the Assizes* Henry II in or about 1166 instituted both the grand assize and the petty assizes of novel disseisin, mort d'ancestor, and utrum, and perhaps others. In a writ of right the issue was who, the demandant or the tenant, had the better right to the tenement. The established method of trial was by battle, but Henry's legislation gave the tenant the privilege of putting himself upon the grand assize, that is, of having the question answered by an assize or inquest composed of twelve lawful knights chosen in the presence of the justices by four knights who had been selected by the sheriff. In the petty assizes the inquest was summoned and sworn to answer the question specified in the writ (there had been no pleadings): In novel disseisin, did the tenant disseise the demandant of the described tenement unjustly and without judgment since the King's last journey to Normandy? In *mort d'ancestor,* did A die seised of the described tenement and was B his nearest heir? Here the issue or issues were definite, but there was no attempt in either a grand assize or a petty assize to limit the assize or jury to matter of fact. The question for decision by these triers, these jurors, was of the same sort as that for decision by battle, ordeal, or oath, or other ritual. And this was doubtless true in other controversies where the issue which was submitted to the inquest or jury was framed by the pleadings after the parties had come before the court. Until the issue was made, the method of trial could not be determined. In the petty assizes, questions incidental to the main issue, which the assize or inquest had not been summoned to answer, but which required an answer if the issue was to be properly determined, frequently arose. These questions, too, were often put to the assize, so that a trial by jury or inquest often involved the determination of several issues. At the same time, as various early judicial records show, the use of the jury was becoming more frequent in actions other than the assizes which involved rights in reality.

*Framing Issues by Oral Pleading* During this period the pleadings were oral, and it seems highly probable that the procedure governing them was similar to that which prevailed in the latter part of Edward I's reign and in the fifteenth century, of which the Year Books give us a vivid picture. By this time there had developed a profession of pleaders, and parties were usually represented or accompanied by counsel. No doubt the same rigid formality of statement in the writ was required; no doubt the same technical phrasing of the claim in conformity with the writ was insisted upon in the declaration as finally drafted, and a corresponding adherence to form in the denial and the other pleas or exceptions, as well, but the proceedings by which the parties, their pleaders or counsel, and the court evolved the precise issue for trial and the phrasing in which it was to be enrolled were informal in the extreme. Thus: The pleader makes his statement of claim or defense. The opponent thinking it insufficient interposes, "Judgment of that." The court may turn to the pleader and demand, "Say something else," or reply to the objector, "Say something." Or there may be a debate between counsel or between counsel and court. Biting remarks by the court, sometimes punctuated by profanity, are not uncommon. Counsel, before accepting the court's intimation that his pleading is insufficient or that he must respond to the opponent, may ask time to consult and advise his client. Occasionally in complying he may remark that had the client followed his advice, he would have stood upon his original position. When the substance of the opposing statements has been agreed upon, the language in which they shall be enrolled has to be determined. Holdsworth agrees with Reeves, and the text of the Year Books seems to justify them, that all the statements of parties and pleaders were regarded as tentative until the pleader had put himself "upon such grounds as he could trust. When he finally rested his cause, that was entered upon the roll and abided the judgment of an inquest or the court according as it was a point of law or fact."

When and by what process oral pleadings were superseded by written pleadings is to some extent a matter of conjecture. But it is clear that in the transition period the exchange and filing of paper pleadings were not sufficient. The pleadings had to be presented orally before the justices and their form and content determined in open court, and the paper pleadings had to be made to conform to the proper standards for enrollment.

*The Verdict Contrasted with Ordeal, Battle, and the Like*

At this stage of development, then, the plaintiff, by production of his secta or by some other means of corroboration, must show that he had a claim of sufficient substance to merit a trial; and there followed a pretrial hearing or series of hearings to determine the precise question to which the trial would furnish the answer. That question had to be so phrased as to meet the technical requirements of the long-established practice. When trial was by one of the older methods—ordeal, battle, oath, or other ritual—it was the formulation of the ultimate issue that was all important. When that was done, the legitimate activities of the parties and their representatives were finished, for if the prescribed formalities of trial were strictly observed, divine interposition would guarantee the correct result. There was no need to discriminate between matter of so-called fact and matter of law, between perceptual knowledge and inferred knowledge. It was of no consequence that in the writ of right, the result of the battle determined both fact and law.

But when the knights in the grand assize had to answer who, the demandant or the tenant, had the better right to the tenement, and when the members of the petty assizes had to determine not only what the demandant had done but whether this constituted a disseisin, unjustly and without judgment, or not only what the observable situation was at A's death but whether this situation constituted seisin of Blackacre by A, or not only what was B's apparent connection with A's family, but whether B was A's nearest heir, new problems were presented. There was no place for divine interposition. The whole basis for reference to these men was their supposed familiarity with the facts, their possession of reliable knowledge acquired by their own observation or from persons of undoubted trustworthiness. There was no assumption that they had special skill or knowledge of the law. The same was true where the issue was determined by the pleadings and not fixed in the writ.

*Procedural Consequences of Infirmities of Jurors* Though trial by the assize or by jury seems originally to have been regarded as on the same footing as trial by one of the older methods, with the same finality of result, it could not long remain so. (1) It was too obvious for argument that the kind of question which a body of laymen could satisfactorily answer of their own knowledge or on information obtained from others must have limitations. At the very least, laymen ought not to be required or allowed to determine matters of law. The ultimate question in the litigation might be the same as that in any other form of trial, but the jury or assize must have it broken down for them. (2) It was likewise apparent that a finding of fact by a body of men should not always be accepted as final. They might have been corrupted or mistaken. Jurors should be held responsible for their wrongdoing; and litigants ought to be relieved of the results of any such wrongdoing.

As to the finality of the verdict, it is enough here to point out that the losing litigant was given a remedy at a comparatively early date. He could secure a jury composed of men of higher rank and greater in number, to which the original issue would be submitted. If they gave the same answer as the original jury, well and good. If not, the original jurors were subject to severe penalties for rendering a false verdict and the judgment based on their verdict was set aside and a new judgment entered on the new verdict.

As to matters of law, the verdict was subject to scrutiny on review of the judgment. If the verdict applied a wrong rule of law, it was false and the same consequences followed as if it had been false in fact. Thus, in an assize of novel disseisin in 1224 brought by Martin de Bella Fago against Hugo de Rickingehalle and Roger de Burs (Bracton's *Notebook,* case 917), the jury was punished for a false verdict because it had answered the question submitted on the assumption that as a matter of law a second husband did not have curtesy in his deceased wife's estate, a point upon which the renowned contemporary lawyers, Seagrave and Bracton, held conflicting opinions. For this reason jurors were anxious to be relieved of the obligation to answer questions which involved conclusions of law. They frequently submitted statements of what they knew or had learned from observation and inquiry and asked the aid of the court as to the proper conclusion. The justices frequently, especially in the earlier period, refused to comply, for they were at that time punishable for a false judgment if they mistook the law applicable to the findings. The Statute of Westminster II required the court to receive such special statements in certain assizes and advise the jury whether the facts stated therein did or did not constitute a disseisin.

When the justices ceased to be punishable for a false judgment, they often pointed out that laymen had no understanding of the law and that the pleadings should be so framed that the jurors would concentrate their attention upon the controlling issues of fact. Counsel for one of the parties also is frequently found arguing that he should be permitted in his pleading to set out facts in detail rather than be confined to a statement of the ultimate issue. Often this seems to be due to a fear not that the jurors will mistake the law but that the record will fail to show what was necessarily determined, or that the jurors will lose sight of important matters of fact in reaching the answer to the issue. For example, the plaintiff wants recorded the facts which show that a constitutive document by a predecessor in title disposed not of the predecessor's entire interest but only of a part to which the plaintiff was making no claim. A defendant in place of a flat denial alone wants to set forth facts which constitute a conclusive argumentative denial, making it similar to the inducement which was a necessary part of the later common-law special traverse. The doctrine was soon accepted that the jury was incompetent to pass upon issues of law, and the practice of allowing pleas or exceptions in addition to the flat denial became common.

*Increasing Complexities and Burdens* These measures benefited both the parties and the jurors. They defined more sharply the question which the jurors had to answer, and the jurors had to rely only upon what they knew or had learned of relevant events and conditions, freed from conclusions as to the legal relations resulting from them. They gave the parties redress against manifestly incorrect verdicts. But these advantages were overbalanced by other developments: (1) the expansion of forms of action and the development of technical requirements in statement, and (2) measures designed to liberalize procedure.

*Changes As to Forms of Action and Requirements of Pleading* The resort to the royal courts was increasing and the problems of litigation were becoming more complex. Though the manufacture of new writs was checked by the Provisions of Oxford of 1258 and the Statute of 1285 permitting writs *in consimili casu* was not for a considerable period made use of except in writs of entry, litigants and their counsel were constantly endeavoring to induce the courts to expand the scope of the writs already in the Register. In the fourteenth and fifteenth centuries there is much litigation the result of which depended not on whether counsel had chosen the correct writ but on whether there was any royal writ to fit his case. It was during the 1400s, when the transition from oral to written pleadings was taking place, that the action on the case was coming to be recognized as separate from trespass and counsel were seeking to use it to secure damages for breach of an unsealed promise. Detinue likewise was breaking its original bounds. The first problem of a litigant and his counsel was to select and secure the proper writ, for the writ was the instrument that delegated to the justices the authority to entertain the action. It was of controlling importance. The declaration had to conform to the writ, and to a large degree its language was dictated by the writ. The form of expression thus dictated became as important as the scope of the writ, and a defect of form of statement as fatal as a defect of substance. The task of counsel was calling for greater and greater learning and skill. But these requirements, which may be characterized as technical, could be satisfied without too great difficulty so long as the pleadings were drafted after clarifying discussion by court and counsel before enrollment. And though a jury might be required to answer more than one question in a single action, the questions were clearly framed and comparatively simple. When the transition from oral pleading to written pleading was complete, there was no opportunity for any preliminary discussion or conference which would compel the revelation of the real substance of the conflicting claims of the parties and produce an agreement or decision as to the form in which they should be enrolled. The litigant had to rely solely on the skill of counsel; but when the pleadings were terminated, there was in the earlier stage little doubt, if any, as to the tenor of the question or questions which the jurors had to answer.

*Preparation of Materials for Jury* Under the older forms of trial all the skill and industry of the parties and counsel were exhausted in the framing of the pleadings. There was nothing that they could legitimately do to affect the result of the trial insofar as that was dictated by divine intervention. There was no opportunity to furnish rational support for the desired answer. But the jury had to have rational bases for its answer. Jurors were to rely upon information which they had acquired. What sources of information were open to them? To what extent were the parties and their counsel privileged to supply what under modern conditions we call evidence? In what way did the modern system evolve? How did the development of written pleadings affect the process? Were the burdens of the parties and counsel made more complex and difficult?

First consider the situation when the issue was clearly defined by the pleadings so that both the parties and the jurors at the outset of the trial knew exactly what question or questions of fact had to be answered. The earliest records indicate that the jurors were to make their answer from what they had seen and heard and what they had learned from the words of their fathers and of others whom they were bound to regard as trustworthy. They were never limited to what they had personally perceived, although they were chosen from the vicinage because they were assumed to have reliable information as to the facts. But there was no real insistence that the whole group should come from the scene of the matter in dispute. It was contemplated that jurors could and would inform each other. As to matters concerning which the jurors had, or may have had, no information, the following sources were available:

1. From the earliest times, preappointed witnesses to certain business transactions and witnesses to deeds were summoned with the jury. They retired with the jury;

whether or not in the earlier period they were regarded as virtually members of the jury, it is certain that in the later period they were sworn merely to give information to the jury, and they had no part in the verdict. They performed the functions of modern witnesses but not in open court in the presence of the parties.

2. Each party was entitled to communicate privately with the jurors and give them his version of the facts. There is nothing to indicate that any party had to be given notice or opportunity to be present during such communication; however, Coke seemed to think that this was impliedly required in practice where a party was exercising this privilege pursuant to the Statute of Henry VI, which commanded the sheriff to furnish the names of the jurors at least six days before the session of the court in order that the parties might inform them. Thayer thought Coke mistaken and believed that in the very early period, the parties might privately furnish information to jurors even after they had retired to consider their verdict.

3. Where a sealed document or record was relevant and was pleaded, the only possible question was its authenticity. If that was conceded, the instrument was conclusive. If not, it was exhibited to the jury and was taken to the jury room. Though not pleaded, it could still be exhibited to the jury, in which case it was usually described as evidence, to be considered with other information. Unsealed documents were likewise presented as so-called evidence.

4. The chief source of information furnished at the trial was the statements of counsel for the respective parties. As indicated earlier, counsel endeavored to have as many

details as possible included in the pleadings so as to have them a matter of record and impress them upon the minds of the jurors. When the court refused counsel's request to have a particular statement embodied in the pleadings, counsel was told that he could state it in evidence. And it seems clear that when a serjeant made such a statement, he was vouching his belief in its truth, but, of course, he was not under oath or testifying to it as a matter within his own knowledge.

5. What of persons performing the function of modern witnesses, that is, testifying under oath to matters relevant to the issue? In this connection, reference must be made to the offense of maintenance in the 1400s and the first half of the 1500s. The cases show that a person who volunteered to support another in any litigation in which the supporter was not vouched to warranty or under other obligation of support was subject to punishment for maintenance, and any person who furnished evidence in favor of the litigant which he was not bound to furnish was a maintainer. As early as 1433 a defendant was charged with the offense of maintenance for having attended and given evidence as a witness at the request of one of the parties in an assize of rent. This and some later cases convinced Thayer that the courts were customarily receiving testimony from witnesses comparatively early in the fifteenth century, for the records show the justices making some rather fine distinctions between situations in which a stranger to the litigation may safely testify and those in which the giving of testimony will subject him to punishment. In the latter part of the 1400s, we find witnesses

testifying frequently, but it was not until the reign of Elizabeth that a litigant was entitled to compulsory process for witnesses.

Fortescue, writing probably between 1460 and 1476, describes a trial by jury as beginning with the court reading the record to the jury and explaining to them the issue which they are to decide. Next each party, by himself or his counsel, will state and show to the jurors everything which he thinks relevant to the issue. And then each will present all the witnesses on his side; each of these will be sworn "on the holy evangelists of God" to testify to all he knows upon the matter in issue. Fortescue notes that these witnesses may be examined separately, so that the testimony of one may not instruct the others or induce them to give like testimony. The record of a famous case in 1465 furnishes complete corroboration of Fortescue's story. In an assize of novel disseisin several serjeants—Littleton, Fairfax, and Catesby—appeared for the plaintiff. Each of these, as well as the counsel for defendant, recites at great length (the record says "shows in evidence") a detailed account of the facts, as he contended them to be. In the course of his statement Littleton, who apparently opened, refers to two persons who are present and will testify to particular matters. Yong, for the defendant, makes an extended statement of defendant's version of the facts; he says that the defendant's farmer and rent-collector are present to declare certain things to the court. Then he offers certain documents. So far as the record shows, no witness is actually called to testify until Catesby demands that the farmer testify. Thereafter the farmer and the rent-collector are sworn and examined by the court. Fairfax then tells what occurred at the view. A discussion as to the law follows, after which the court charges the jury, telling them that they have heard much evidence from both sides and that they may, if they so desire, find a special verdict instead of saying precisely disseisin or the contrary.

It is clear, then, that in trial by jury even when the pleadings were required to produce a single issue, the parties and counsel in proper preparation for trial had to assemble part of the relevant data and be familiar with all of them. Most of what they had prepared they could get before the jury by recitation or by the offer of documents, some of it, by the later practice, by testimony of witnesses. The jury, as Fortescue explained, had a fund of knowledge derived from whatever other sources they deemed worthy of consulting. They were not bound to accept what was presented to them in court and could rely upon their otherwise acquired knowledge in reaching their verdict. And Fortescue indicates that the testimony of witnesses was of very minor importance. By the early part of the 1600s, as Coke tells us, the jury was relying principally upon such testimony, but it was not until well into the eighteenth century that the present practice was established.

The system of written pleadings had given the parties and their counsel complete control over the area of dispute, so that occasionally a highly skilled pleader could divert the controversy to a subordinate issue. Yet so long as the courts required the pleadings to produce a single issue or the few issues made by a flat denial of plaintiff's necessary allegations, each so clearly stated that neither party nor counsel could misunderstand it, preparation for trial remained a comparatively simple matter, and the task of the jury relatively easy to perform.

*Effect of Liberalizing Procedure* But, as we all know, the parties were not long restricted to a single issue. By the middle of the 1700s, all semblance of simplicity had been rendered impossible because of the following developments (I make no attempt to list them in chronological order):

1. The requirement of a preliminary showing of merit had vanished. The production of the suit of witnesses had become a fiction.

2. Uncertainty as to the scope of several of the forms of action had appeared, and many of the orthodox allegations were not subject to denial.

3. The courts permitted a plaintiff to join in a single action all the claims which he had against the defendant remediable in the same form of action. As to each claim the pleadings evolved a single issue. Several lawsuits were tried at the same time by the same jury. The reliance upon evidence by strangers increased. Witnesses became subject to compulsory process. Hence the work of preparation by counsel and the task of the jury were more burdensome and complicated, even assuming that each of plaintiff's claims was bona fide.

4. The material submitted to the jury had to sustain the precise issue evolved, and since the pleadings frequently went into detail, a party might well be defeated on the specific issue when he should have won on the merits with

a slightly different statement. Counsel therefore tried the dodge of stating his single cause in as many different ways as he thought the materials available might be interpreted to fit. He pretended that each statement of a ground of recovery was a statement of a completely different cause. Of course, the justices might well have prevented this, but they thought it proper to allow it.

5. The Statute of Anne in 1705 permitted a defendant with leave of court to interpose as many pleas to the merits as he might have. To every statement of a purported cause, that is, to every count in the declaration, several pleas might be pleaded. The subsequent pleadings had to be single so as to produce a single issue on each plea. But to the general issue there was no response save a joinder of issue.

6. The defenses admissible under the general issue varied with the form of action. In debt on a simple contract, the general issue by its terms permitted negative and affirmative defenses. In the action on the case, it permitted defendant to prove defenses by way of excuse or discharge as well as denial, for this action was treated as if plaintiff were asserting that upon all the facts as they existed at the commencement of the action, he was entitled to recover.

7. When in 1602 Slade's Case permitted an action of assumpsit on a fictitious promise to pay a preexisting simple contract debt, and when thereafter its doctrine was expanded to include all situations where defendant had money for which in equity and good conscience he was obliged to account to plaintiff, a Pandora's box was opened. The declaration in general assumpsit gave no information

as to the transaction or event on which plaintiff relied as creating the fictitious promise, and if defendant pleaded the general issue, he gave plaintiff no information as to the defense upon which he intended in fact to rely.

In some forms of action, the pleadings did still reveal the real issue. But on the whole the system of common-law pleading which the judges and lawyers developed defeated the very purpose which it should have served. It had become an art requiring infinite care as to form and encouraging subtlety of scholastic reasoning, but affording neither court nor parties notice as to the issues of fact which would be the subject of proof at the trial. And this at a time when such notice had become essential because the chief source of the information upon which the jury based its verdict was matter presented to them in open court by the parties. Adequate preparation for trial required the investigation of all materials relevant to any state of facts which a lively legal imagination could conceive as possibly relevant under each of a series of issues. To call such pleading issue pleading was to ignore actualities. It was a far cry indeed from the simplicity of issue and disclosure in advance of trial of the real area of dispute which prevailed in the days of oral pleading.

*The English Hilary Rules* I need not remind you of the futility of the attempt to induce the English Bench to cure these evils. The Hilary Rules did something towards compelling disclosure by the pleadings of the points really in dispute, but they were interpreted to require a nicety in form of statement which baffled all but the most erudite.

Before they went into effect one case in six turned on the pleadings without regard to the merits, under their influence, one in four. It was the failure of this English experiment that caused American reformers to turn to the legislature and to attempt to make written pleadings perform the function of the early oral pleading in the modern setting—where on the common-law side most trials were by a jury which must base its verdict on evidence presented in court and on instructions as to the law given by the court. First, they desired to do away with all technical restrictions caused by the writ system and forms of action. Next, they wanted to confine the function of jurors to matters of fact as distinguished from law. This meant that the pleadings must assert propositions of fact only, and in framing them, the pleader should use plain language without unnecessary repetition. He should not plead evidence on the one hand, or bare legal conclusions on the other. The pleadings should reveal the respective states of facts which the pleaders contended to have existed. Although the Field Code in New York and those which copied its provisions cut the pleadings off with the reply, it was believed that complaint, answer, and reply properly drawn would reveal the essence of the factual controversy so that neither party would be subject to surprise at the trial, and there would be little, if any, quibbling about the form of statement.

*Code Pleading* The dreams of the codifiers might have come true had Jack Cade's recipe been followed and complemented by burning all the law books. But in some states, not excluding New York, theory of pleading was invented to perform the function of the old writ; the ghost of the buried form of action haunted Bench and Bar. A material averment in the form of a conclusion of law was held to be insufficient. The codifiers evidently thought a statement of law easily distinguishable from a statement of fact. But experience has shown that many courts, though they believe the distinction all-important, are still unable to draw the distinguishing line. What one court calls an allowable statement of fact, another condemns as a conclusion of law. The Field Code was adopted in 1848, but it was not until 1920 that the Court of Appeals held that an allegation that a promise was "for a valuable consideration" was not an allegation of law, thus resolving a conflict which had theretofore existed between decisions of the inferior courts. The original Field Code contained 391 sections; by 1919 it had grown to more than 3,400 sections. It used to be said that the average lawyer learned it at $10.00 a section —the cost of permission to amend. Charles Boston at one time estimated that one third of the time of the New York courts was consumed in deciding mere matters of procedure. There is still under the Practice Act opportunity for much haggling and delay in deciding objections to mere matters of form.

But my fundamental objection to the typical code is that a party can comply with its terms and keep hidden his real ground of attack or defense. In this way he can put his opponent to needless expense involved in preparation to meet issues that will not actually be litigated. Without some provision for discovery much more extensive than that allowed in the usual nonstatutory bill, a defendant by general denial and stock affirmative defenses can in the ordinary case put plaintiff to the necessity of useless preparation. Complaints are drafted before adequate investigation of the facts, either in very general language which will permit the use of any possibly discoverable evidence, or with statements of details that may possibly be discovered before trial. If a plaintiff's general allegation is met by a motion to make more definite and certain, he alleges every specification which a fertile imagination can conceive as possible in the pertinent situation, with the result that the defendant knows no more as to what will be actually litigated than he did before the motion was made. Had the lawyers and judges received the code with a determination to make it produce the result that the codifiers had intended, it would doubtless have given us a simplified procedure by which controversies could be adjusted with reasonable speed and without undue expense. But they were unwilling or unable to do so.

*Notice Pleading* Notice pleading has been suggested as a remedy for eliminating quibbling over pleading. Motions directed at the pleadings are taboo. A very general statement reveals the subject of the controversy and the claim. Under the so-called German-Italian system in vogue after the First World War, as described by an American observer, the defendant received the first detailed information in plaintiff's opening statement. He was expected to disclose his defense in his oral response. In theory these statements would reveal the nub of the controversy. Surprise by either party was made harmless by a continuance. But the theory neglected to reckon with the tactical objectives of counsel and the practical problems of the judge. Counsel desired always to keep his hand hidden. The court desired always to have the issue limited so as to shorten the time of trial. The result was, as a German trial judge once informed me, that before the case was ready for trial, sometimes ten or a dozen exchanges of opening statements, with accompanying continuances, were required. And it needs little or no imagination to foresee what would probably happen in the average American jurisdiction. What it would amount to would be a series of pretrial hearings that would be even more expensive and time-consuming than the procedure under the code.

The great merit of the ancient system of oral pleading was the disclosure under the supervision of the court of the exact question to be answered at the trial. Neither party nor the court could be taken by surprise. The unfortunate development of intricacies of pleading and the abandonment of all attempt by the court to limit the paper issue to what was really in controversy, coupled with the development of trial by jury and the use of evidence, led to the situation where the needless expenditure of time and money was required first, to comply with the technical requirements of statement and counterstatement and second, to guard against surprise at the trial by investigation and acquisition of available evidence on all possibly relevant matters. No doubt reform movements here and in England and piecemeal legislation have made impossible or unprofitable many captious objections to pleadings, but all efforts to compel disclosure of each party's case in the pleadings have signally failed.

*Federal Rules* It was against this background of experience that the Federal Rules of Civil Procedure were drafted. They frankly abandon all attempt to make a party show his hand in his pleadings. The system which they set up is not notice pleading, nor is it fact pleading as under the typical code. Great generality of statement is permitted. Even the common counts of the common-law system are allowed. A pleading good under the code is certainly sufficient under the rules, but many a pleading which would be condemned under a typical code would pass muster under the rules. They try to lessen the opportunity for delay caused by fighting over pleadings by limiting the opportunity for attack. They abolish bills of particulars. A motion to make more definite and certain is unavailing if the pleading is sufficient to enable the opponent to draft his response. Free amendment and the privilege of the judge to allow a party to change an attack on the pleadings into a motion for summary judgment make it practically impossible for a party to secure a judgment which disregards the merits.

In the absence of provisions for adequate discovery, these rules of pleading would, in my opinion, be unworkable under modern conditions. It is a commonplace that lawsuits are won or lost before trial. This means only that the lawyer who goes to trial without thorough preparation on both law and facts is bound to lose unless his opponent has been guilty of equal or greater negligence. And no proper investigation of either law or fact can be made without a clear comprehension of the objective. Unless the states of fact which may appear at the trial are known, preparation of the applicable law is impossible. The pleadings under the rules may be so drawn as not to reveal matters which the pleader hopes his opponent will not be prepared to meet. The relevant facts or evidence of them may lie in documents or in tangible objects, or merely within the minds of individuals. Counsel may have to start with nothing more than the statement of his client or the allegations in a pleading. But under the rules he has at hand the means of securing all available information. Rules 26 to 37, if properly used, will enable each party to know exactly what the other claims to be the pertinent facts and what are all the sources of available evidence known to the other. In this search he will not be hampered by the exclusionary rules of evidence. The use of Federal Rules 33 and 36 will involve no more expense in the usual case than would the drafting and arguing of a motion for a more definite statement in a pleading. Rule 33 provides that each party may submit to the other questions concerning any matter relevant to the subject matter involved in the action, including the existence, description, nature, custody, condition, and location of any books, documents, or other tangibles and the identity and location of persons having knowledge of the facts. Obviously, no party has ever been required, in response to any sort of motion, to set forth such details in a pleading. The answers to the questions must be under oath and the questions cannot be ignored without a substantial penalty. Rule 36 authorizes a party to request the opponent to admit in writing the authenticity of any relevant document or the truth of any relevant proposition of fact. Unless the matter called for is privileged, the opponent must make the admission or show good cause why he cannot do so. He cannot ignore the request as he can under most similar code provisions. These two provisions will produce all the information which a party can need to begin a thorough investigation of his opponent's claim or defense. The answers and admissions will disclose all facts known to the opposing party. Matters not within his knowledge may be learned by taking depositions and requiring the production of documents and opportunity for inspection of relevant places and things.

It has been objected that the objectives of Rules 33 and 36 may be defeated by having counsel draft the responses ambiguously or with cleverly phrased qualifications. Provisions for the protection of deponents against improper questioning may be perverted to cause undue expense and delay and defeat the very purpose of the discovery process. It might be answered that at worst the result will be more desirable than that which could be obtained under the orthodox code practice. A better answer is that if the first responses to the questions submitted or to the request for admissions are unsatisfactory, another set of questions or requests may be made, so drafted as to prevent repetition of the defects in the former, and the court can prevent the use of devices to defeat or unduly prolong the effective taking of depositions. But there is no dodging the obvious truth. If the Bench and Bar are determined to make the rules unworkable, they will soon be construed into nothingness. If the Bar is recalcitrant but the Bench determined to enforce the rules, they will slowly become effective. If both Bench and Bar accept them as an instrument for making the trial of the case a proceeding for the speedy determination of litigation, they will soon accomplish their purpose. The Bench and Bar can make a cumbrous machine turn out a satisfactory product; they can also so operate a first-class machine as to produce inferior goods. A code-state lawyer who examines the paper procedural establishment in New Hampshire would expect to find a group of decisions characteristic of England in the eighteenth century or of Illinois in the nineteenth and the twentieth prior to the Practice Act: separate courts of law and equity, though with the same personnel; forms of action on the law side; the usual provisions for disregard of technical defects and freedom of amendment, usually also construed as accomplishing nothing. But if he inquires further, he will find that the courts have not been hampered by forms of action; they do not hesitate to permit an amendment from an action in general assumpsit to an action of trespass or case for wrongful death. If during the trial of a law case, it appears that the action should have been brought in equity, the court discharges the jury and the trial continues as if the proper procedure had been employed originally. The statute for discovery has been liberally construed. The Bar has used it extensively and has made its use inexpensive by stipulations concerning the time, place, and manner of taking depositions, their use at the trial, and the making of transcripts. The success or failure of any procedural device depends upon the judges and lawyers who have the privilege or duty of using it.

Not only do the rules provide for disclosure of the materials relevant to the controversy; they provide also for their use to eliminate fictitious issues. No longer can a party hope to succeed by denial of an allegation which he knows to be true, because he thinks his opponent will be unable to produce admissible evidence of its truth. Rule 16 authorizes a pretrial hearing. If proper advantage has been taken of the discovery provisions, there will be available to the judge and the parties material which will disclose what elements of the case are the subject of bona fide dispute; and these only will be reserved for trial. Though Rule 16 makes the holding of a pretrial hearing discretionary with the judge, most federal district judges make pretrial hearings a part of the regular routine. Where a party believes himself entitled to a summary judgment, he can in effect compel a pretrial hearing by a motion under Rule 56. And at this hearing, if the judge obeys the mandate of the rule, he will "if practicable, ascertain what material facts exist without substantial controversy and what material facts are actually and in good faith controverted" and "make an order specifying the facts that appear without substantial controversy, including the extent to which the amount of damages or other relief is not in controversy, and directing such further proceedings in the action as are just." If he does so, then "upon the trial of the action the facts so specified shall be deemed established, and the trial shall be conducted accordingly."

There is now available to the Bench and Bar a procedure by which litigants can secure all the advantages of the Year Book system of oral pleading without its disadvantages; where form of statement is of negligible importance and there need be no controversy over matters not in bona fide dispute; where all available relevant information can be known to both parties before trial and each party can guard against surprise by making adequate preparation upon the merits of the actual dispute under the applicable rules of law.

It is doubtless true that the theory of our adversary system is attractive in statement. It may be the best we can devise, but it seldom fits the facts in modern litigation. If it were to operate perfectly, both parties would have the same opportunities and capacities for investigation, including the resources to finance them, equal facilities for producing all the discoverable materials, equal good or bad fortune with reference to availability of witnesses and preservation of evidence, and equal persuasive skill in the presentation of evidence and argument. The case is rare where there is even approximate equality in these respects, and there is no practical method of providing it. But there can be no question that the system ought to enable each litigant in advance to know the exact area of dispute and to have access to all available data, so that he may be aware in just what particulars he and his adversary disagree, that he may investigate and determine the pertinency and value of any materials favorable or unfavorable to his contention, and that he may consider the reliability of the persons willing or compellable to testify. Until he knows what state or states of fact the trier may find, he cannot prepare upon the substantive law. Until he knows what evidence is likely to be available for or against him, he cannot prepare to meet or interpose objections under the complex rules governing competency of witnesses, privileges of parties and witnesses, and the admissibility of unprivileged relevant evidence. So long as a party may divert the inquiry from the elements bona fide in dispute, or conceal the real crux of his claim or defense, and thereby take his opponent by surprise, so long will the description of a trial as a battle of wits between contending counsel have a large measure of truth, and a distinguished judge like Jerome Frank may with much justification express the opinion that a lawsuit is a game of chance. The first step toward making a lawsuit a rational proceeding for discovering the factual basis of a controversy is acceptance of these provisions of the Federal Rules. The next is a complete renovation of the rules of evidence.

# JUDICIAL NOTICE

I

In discussing the doctrine of judicial notice, I have the temerity to disagree with the two great masters of the law of evidence, James Bradley Thayer and John Henry Wigmore —with both, as to its nature as an essential constituent of our system of administering justice, and with Wigmore, as to its place in the judicial process. My basic propositions are (1) that our tribunals for administering justice are erected for the sole purpose of adjusting as between litigants disputes affecting their legal relations, and (2) that an essential qualification for membership in such a tribunal is knowledge of certain matters and the capacity to apply it by the usual processes of reasoning to the problems properly presented for solution. Corollaries of these propositions are (1) that the matters thus known, that is, judicially noticed, are indisputable, and (2) that knowledge of them is applicable throughout the judicial process from beginning to end. The judicial authorities support these propositions, but they also reveal the need for reasonable safeguards against the misuse of judicial notice.

Let me begin with a consideration or restatement of a few elementary propositions.

1. For the purpose of procuring an orderly, rational adjustment of controversies affecting legal rights and duties,

Government provides a tribunal of first instance with the power to decide both disputes as to facts and disputes as to the tenor and applicability of rules of law, and other tribunals with limited power to review its decisions. The common-law tribunal of first instance consists of an expert in the law, a judge, and a group of nonexperts, representative of the citizens of the community, a jury. In so far as the dispute concerns the tenor or applicability of a rule of law, the decision, under modern conditions, is for the judge alone.[1] A dispute as to facts is for the decision of the jury acting under the supervision of the judge. This allocation of functions between judge and jury serves as a controlling guide for the judge in equity, where there normally is no jury, and in a common-law case where a jury is waived.

2. The dispute must be one affecting legal rights and duties—not one which concerns interests not subject to legal protection—and it must be a genuine dispute. The tribunal has no power to entertain a collusive action, or one to determine how a real dispute which has been settled by the parties would have been decided had they litigated it, or one to determine what, if any, legal relations would be or would have been created in an imagined situation.

3. The tribunal does not initiate action of its own motion. It has no knowledge of the existence or tenor of a controversy until the controversy is brought to its attention by one or more of the parties. It has no machinery for investigating the facts relevant to the dispute. The parties are required to furnish the materials for decision of matters

[1] In many states the jury is the judge of both law and fact in prosecutions for criminal libel and, in a few states, in all criminal prosecutions.

of fact, and the judge determines which of the parties must make what facts known to the tribunal; that is to say, he declares what the court will assume to be the facts upon each issue in the absence of evidence of a specified quantity and quality to the contrary. As to the law, the situation is entirely different. The judge is charged with the duty of knowing the law of the forum—the domestic law. Knowledge of that law and its applicability to any issue presented for decision, or the capacity to acquire and use that knowledge, is a requisite of the office. Whether he has it or not, he must be assumed to have it. He may call upon the parties to assist him, but when all is said and done, what knowledge he has must pass for what he ought to have. If he is mistaken, he may perhaps be corrected by a higher court, which, if a court of last resort, for all practical purposes cannot be mistaken.

4. In dealing with an issue as to the tenor or applicability of a rule of law, the judge is free to make such investigation as he sees fit. He may rely upon or ignore briefs of counsel for the contending parties; he may consult such sources of information as his judgment or fancy suggests. He may think a passage from Shakespeare or a fable from Aesop more persuasive than an opinion of the United States Supreme Court. He may make no investigation at all and rely upon a judicial hunch, or upon what he already knows or thinks he knows. In all this, he is in no way subject to the control of the parties. He may seek assistance of them and their counsel, but he may reject all advice offered by them and rely upon sources not revealed to them. He may reach a conclusion contrary to all previous judicial deci-

sions. The only remedy of a party aggrieved by the result is resort to a reviewing tribunal—an appellate court—and his grievance cannot rest upon any supposed improper use of sources of investigation.

The usual statement of this duty and function of the judge is that the judge must take judicial notice of the domestic law, and subject to the rule against invited error, no request from a party is necessary. Rule 801 of the American Law Institute Model Code and Rule 9 of the Uniform Rules of Evidence are phrased in terms of mandatory judicial notice without request. No objection can be made to this terminology, for it describes the qualification of the judge and by implication distinguishes what he does or may know from what he must be assumed to know. It also connotes his freedom from restriction in the process of acquiring the information which will make the assumption come true. Both the assumption and the process are essential to the Anglo-American system. The functions of the judicial office in that system cannot be performed on any other basis.

5. On the other hand, where the issue presented is the truth or falsity of a disputable and disputed proposition of fact, the assumption and process are entirely different. The assumption is that the tribunal begins with no knowledge as to the truth or falsity of the proposition and that it is restricted to the use of materials presented in court in resolving the issue. Neither the judge nor the jury is permitted to make an independent investigation. The investigation has been made by the parties and they will offer such portions of the result of the investigation as they deem

advisable. Many relevant discovered items may be withheld through ignorance or design, and many others may have been undiscovered through negligence. Of the relevant material offered much may be excluded on objection based on recognized rules of evidence and procedure. As Michael and Adler have made clear, the trier of fact must base his finding upon what happens in his presence in court. On analysis all he knows is that each witness has uttered a series of sounds which seem to him to form words intended to convey a specified idea or series of ideas, or that certain writings received in evidence appear to him to contain symbols that form words and thereby convey certain ideas or that certain objects appear to have certain qualities. From these experiences of perception he must determine the ideas intended to be conveyed and whether they conform to what actually happened or existed. The trier of fact is not charged with the duty of knowing or discovering the truth of the disputed proposition, or even what appears to be the truth which would be disclosed by all available data, but merely to find, for the purpose of resolving this controversy between these litigants, the truth or falsity of the proposition as it appears from the materials submitted. In short, from what the trier has perceived during the course of the trial, he must deduce what probably happened in the past and in some instances what is likely to happen in the future. He cannot even begin this process without reasoning, and he cannot reason without reliance upon his past experiences. If the trier is the judge, he cannot be treated as if ignorant of what is so generally accepted as to be incapable of dispute among reasonable men; he must be assumed to have that fund of general information which is common to all reasonably well-informed persons in the community. That fund will consist of knowledge of generalizations and of specific facts. He must also have the capacity to relate this knowledge to what he has perceived during the trial and to draw conclusions from the combination by the ordinary processes of thought. All this is true also when the trier is a jury with a judge presiding. As a practical matter, the fund of general information of jurors will often be less than that of the judge, but if so, it can be supplemented by the judge in his charge.

In terms of judicial notice, the court, which includes both judge and jury, must take judicial notice of what everyone knows and uses in the ordinary process of reasoning about everyday affairs. Unless this were assumed our system of trial would collapse. Without such an assumption, a rational resolution of a dispute by a trier of fact, based upon data submitted by others, is impossible.

II

To this tribunal thus equipped, furnished by Government to resolve disputes as to law and fact, the adversary parties present the questions to be determined. Though they have a large measure of control in defining the area of controversy, they are subject to limitations imposed by the very purpose for which the tribunal is created. They cannot insist that it decide frivolous disputes. If a pleading is on its face so obviously bad that no respectable lawyer would consider its validity to be even arguable, it will be stricken; on the other hand, if it is so clearly valid that no respectable argument can be framed against its validity, a demurrer to it or other form of attack upon it will be rejected as frivolous. In like manner an allegation in a pleading contrary to what is so clearly true as to be incapable of dispute among reasonable men will be disregarded, and no evidence in support of it will be received.

It goes without saying that the tenor of a specified rule of law cannot be allowed to vary from case to case or be made to depend upon the superiority in diligence or skill of counsel of one of the parties as compared to that of his opponent. It is equally true that a decision as to facts contrary to what is so generally accepted as the truth as to be incapable of dispute among reasonable men cannot be tolerated. In the practical operation of our adversary system, where so much does in fact depend upon the financial resources of the respective parties and the comparative diligence, skill and other qualities of contending counsel, it is especially important that a party be prevented from perverting the true function of the court by presenting a moot issue or securing a wrong result by disputing what is demonstrably indisputable among reasonable persons. Just as the court cannot fulfill the purpose of its creation unless the judge knows the law, and unless both judge and jury have the fund of information possessed by all reasonably intelligent men in the community and, in addition, the capacity to use the ordinary processes of rational thought, so the court will be diverted from its duty to adjust legal relations between litigants if it permits the parties to dispute the indisputable, to take issue upon and secure results contrary to either what is so notoriously true as not to be subject to reasonable dispute or what is capable of immediate and accurate demonstration by resort to sources of indisputable accuracy easily accessible to the court. To allow the court to be thus diverted would be to destroy the very reason for its existence. And it is to prevent this diversion and to accomplish the objective of its creation that it takes notice of indisputable matters of fact. This, I submit, is the secure foundation upon which judicial notice of matters of fact is built.

It is at this point that I am in opposition to the great masters, though I have the support of the American Law Institute and the Uniform Commissioners. To justify my position I must, first, harmonize it with a generally recognized rule and, second, must consider the judicial authorities which appear to accept the views of Thayer and Wigmore.

1. The generally recognized rule is that there are some matters of fact which a court may, but need not, judicially notice. If a matter is indisputable it is within the domain of judicial notice. How then can a court be justified in failing or refusing to notice it? If it is disputable, it falls into the field of evidence and cannot be judicially noticed. It must be either disputable or indisputable; how, then, can there be any intermediate ground? The answer is the resultant of three other universally accepted propositions: (1) under our system of litigation a party has no right to complain of error in a trial court's action if he was responsible for inducing it or if he failed to take the prescribed procedural measures to prevent it; (2) the personal knowledge of the judge or the jurors or counsel may

not be coextensive with the judicial knowledge of the judge; and (3) whether or not the truth of a given proposition is disputable may itself be the subject of a dispute among reasonable men.

The best illustration of the first proposition is found in cases where there is universal agreement that the matter in question must be judicially noticed, namely, the law of the forum. In the *Great American Ins. Co. v. Glenwood Irrigation Company*,[2] the Court of Appeals for the Eighth Circuit held that a party was not entitled to the benefit of an applicable statute because he had not called it to the court's attention. On the other hand, in the Glebe Sugar Refining Case[3] the House of Lords reversed the lower courts because their decisions were in conflict with a statutory provision which was first brought into the case by one of the Law Lords after the close of the original argument. No mention of the provision, to say nothing of reliance upon it, had previously occurred. The conflict between these two cases is due to the difference of opinion concerning the obligations of counsel for the parties. Again, in Connecticut an applicable statute expressly put the burden of pleading and proving contributory negligence upon the defendant, but the Supreme Court held that a plaintiff by pleading due care had invited the court to put upon him the burden of proving it,[4] and in a later case held, in effect, that the trial judge must accept the invitation.[5] There was no intimation that the judge need

[2] 265 F. 594 (C.A. 8th, 1920).
[3] [1921] A.C. 66.
[4] Boyd v. Geary, 126 Conn. 396, 12 A.2d 644 (1940).
[5] Hatch v. Merigold, 119 Conn. 339, 176 Atl. 266 (1935).

not judicially know the terms of the statute or that he did not have personal knowledge of it. The plaintiff's pleading made that knowledge immaterial, for it made the statute inapplicable. The courts which hold otherwise do so because they are unwilling to accept Connecticut's bizarre concept of an invitation to error. There is, however, pretty general agreement that a party who conducts the trial on the theory that one specified rule of law is applicable to the exclusion of another cannot complain that the judge accepted that theory and shift to the other theory on appeal.

2. As to the conscious knowledge of the judge of a matter of fact, which is so notorious as to be indisputable, it is too clear to require argument that much may depend upon conditions at the place of trial. Consequently a greater amount of discretion must be accorded to the trial judge. The case of *Varcoe v. Lee*[6] has been highly commended as an instructive example. There the matter of fact was that the property fronting on Mission Street between Twentieth and Twenty-second Streets in San Francisco was occupied by structures devoted to business. A judge resident in San Francisco and every reasonably well-informed resident would know this fact, and at a trial in a California state court sitting in San Francisco, it would be judicially noticed. If the case were being tried in an Eastern state, there would be no common knowledge of the fact. The same might well be true if the trial were held in another part of California. Even in a court held in San Francisco a particular judge assigned to try the case might have no

[6] Varcoe v. Lee, 180 Cal. 338, 181 Pac. 223 (1919).

knowledge and might rule that in the absence of pertinent information to be furnished by one of the parties, he would require evidence and treat the fact as subject to dispute.

Concerning the reasonableness of a dispute as to whether a matter is indisputable, I have been able to find no decision so apt as that in *State v. Damm.*[7] There the defendant was indicted for a rape, the result of which was the birth of a child to the prosecutrix. The defendant sought an order that samples of blood of the mother and child be furnished in order that experts might determine the blood group of each and compare it with that of defendant. He asked the court to take judicial notice that the blood group of a child is determined by that of its parents, and that where the blood of the child contains no characteristic of the blood of the alleged father, it is impossible that the child should have been begotten by him. The judge refused the request, and the Supreme Court of South Dakota in October, 1931, held that he had not abused his discretion in so ruling.

On rehearing, in April, 1936, it declared its "considered opinion" to be "that the reliability of the blood test is definitely, and indeed unanimously, established as a matter of expert scientific opinion entertained by authorities in the field." It nevertheless reaffirmed the trial court's ruling, saying:

> This case was tried in October, 1931. As will be noted from the citations earlier set forth, the literature of the topic of the scientific reliability of the blood test (at least the body of such literature available in the English language) is, for the most part, subsequent to that date. We are far from willing to say that it

[7] 64 S.D. 309, 266 N.W. 667 (1936).

was error for a trial judge in South Dakota, at the time of the trial of this case, to fail or refuse to take judicial notice of such reliability, notwithstanding the fact that by the assistance of able counsel, and from our own subsequent investigations, we have arrived at a complete belief in such reliability. If such reliability was not, at the time of the trial of this case, a matter which the trial court was obligated judicially to notice, then it was necessary for the applicant for the order to prove such reliability by proper and satisfactory expert testimony. Only one witness was called to the point, and his testimony in regard thereto was vague, indefinite, and unconvincing. We are equally unwilling to say that the learned trial judge erred in failing or refusing to accept such testimony as a sufficient basis for the making of the requested order. In other words, the reliability of the test (conceding our own present conviction that such reliability does exist as a matter of scientific fact) "does not sufficiently appear from the record in this case," which is the precise point upon which we sought to base our previous opinion, as hereinbefore pointed out.

The material upon which the court relied would not have been admissible under the rules of evidence, and most of it was not available to the trial judge. The proposition was intrinsically as indisputable in 1931 as in 1936. The sources of indubitable accuracy, however, were not readily available in South Dakota at that time, and the parties did not provide them. To a judge in the position of the trial judge, furnished only with the data produced by the parties, the matter appeared to be within the realm of dispute among reasonable men, and he was right in requiring it to be proved.

The converse of *State v. Damm* is found in the judicial history of the doctrine that a woman is capable of childbearing during her entire adult life. This was originally taken to be so universally true that it was established as a rule of property. The Supreme Court of the United States taking judicial notice of the developments of modern surgery and the Court of Appeals for the Second Circuit later taking notice of statistics compiled by the United States Department of Commerce in effect removed this matter of fact from the category of the indisputable to that of the disputable.[8]

The American Law Institute and the Uniform Commissioners were, therefore, wise in providing that if the information available to the judge, whether or not furnished by the parties, fails to convince him that the matter is within the realm of judicial notice he shall refuse to notice it judicially. The decisions upholding a court's apparent or real failure or refusal to take judicial notice of an indisputable matter are explainable by the conditions which our adversary system of litigation imposes on the processes of investigation and demonstration, the limitations educational and otherwise of judges, jurors, and counsel and the practical difficulties of securing access to sources of indisputable accuracy containing the relevant data.

A necessary deduction from my position is that if a fact lies within the field of judicial notice, no evidence tending to prove its contrary is admissible. Thayer's statement to the contrary is:

Taking judicial notice does not import that the matter is indisputable. It is not necessarily anything more than a *prima facie* recognition, leaving the matter still open to controversy. It is true,

[8] United States v. Provident Trust Co., 291 U.S. 272 (1934); City Bank Farmers' Trust Co. v. United States, 74 F.2d 692 (C.C.A. 2d 1935).

as regards many of the things which are judicially noticed, that they cannot well be supposed to admit of question: *e.g.*, that Missouri is east of the Rocky Mountains, and that Hereford borders on Wales; but the doctrine covers much else. A seal which purports to be the great seal of any State may in fact not be genuine, and so of the certificate and seal of any public official. A sale of tobacco and cigars may be made for medical purposes, although ordinarily it is not. In very many cases, then, taking judicial notice of a fact is merely presuming it, *i.e.*, assuming it until there shall be reason to think otherwise.[9]

Wigmore[10] says:

That a matter is judicially noticed means merely that it is taken as true without the offering of evidence by the party who should ordinarily have done so. This is because the Court *assumes* that the matter is so notorious that it will not be disputed. But the *opponent is not prevented from disputing* the matter by evidence, if he believes it disputable. It is true that occasionally a Court is found declaring a thing judicially noticed and at the same time refusing to listen to evidence to the contrary; but usually this is in truth laying down a new rule of substantive law by declaring certain facts immaterial; whenever a Court forbids the production of evidence, it removes the subject from the realm of the law of evidence properly so called.

For the proposition that contrary evidence may be offered he cites only *People v. Mayes*[11] from California and *State v. Kincaid*[12] from Oregon, and for the proposition that the refusal to receive evidence amounts to a declaration of substantive law, the Massachusetts case concerning the

[9] THAYER, A PRELIMINARY TREATISE ON EVIDENCE AT THE COMMON LAW 308 (1898).
[10] 9 WIGMORE, EVIDENCE §2567 (3d ed. 1940).
[11] 113 Cal. 618, 45 Pac. 860 (1896).
[12] 133 Ore. 95, 285 Pac. 1105 (1930).

sale of tobacco as a medicine, to which Thayer also refers.[13]

First, consider Thayer's statement. He practically concedes that it would be futile to offer evidence that Missouri lies west of the Rocky Mountains. His treatment of judicial notice concerning official seals and the sale of tobacco and cigars indicates that he misconceives the tenor of the matter noticed. Certainly to say that the court judicially knows the Seal of State of the Commonwealth of Massachusetts does not mean that it judicially knows that the wafer attached to a document or the impression upon the wafer or upon the document is the genuine seal of the Commonwealth, or that the wafer was attached or the impression made by an officer of the Commonwealth acting as such. The court does judicially know the physical appearance of the seal and whether or not the purported seal attached to or impressed on a specified document is in physical appearance identical with that of the genuine seal—this and nothing more. The fact that it judicially knows concerning the sale of tobacco and cigars is that they are not usually sold for medical purposes or upon a physician's prescription, not that they cannot be thus sold.

The same looseness of statement of the content of the matter noticed occurs in numerous other situations. For example, in *Davis v. Farmers Co-operative Equity Co.*,[14] Mr. Justice Brandeis said: "Facts of which we, also, take judicial notice, indicate that the burden upon interstate commerce imposed specifically by the statute here assailed is a heavy one and the obstruction to commerce must be

[13] Commonwealth v. Marzynski, 149 Mass. 68, 21 N.E. 228 (1889).
[14] 262 U.S. 312, 315 (1923).

serious." A footnote to this sentence states that a message of the governor of Minnesota to the legislature recites that an examination of the district court calendars in sixty-seven out of eighty-seven counties disclosed 1,028 pending personal injury cases in which nonresident plaintiffs were seeking damages of nearly $26,000,000 from foreign railroads not operating any line within Minnesota. Of what fact was he taking judicial notice? Certainly if the issue were the exact number of pending cases, the number could not be thus determined. What the court judicially noticed was (1) the existence and content of the official message of the governor to the legislature, and (2) that this official document was evidence that the number of imported actions was so large as to cause the governor to call the matter to the attention of the legislature with a view to remedial legislation. Likewise when Judge Augustus N. Hand[15] took notice of the statistics compiled by the United States Department of Commerce as to the number of births between 1923 and 1932, stating the ages of the mothers, he was not judicially noticing that no woman over fifty-five years of age had during that period borne a child nor even that no such birth had been reported but that the official statistics showed none. From this he drew the conclusion that the proposition that every woman over fifty-five years of age is capable of childbearing should no longer be deemed indisputable. So also the Supreme Court of Florida in using statistics gathered by various official and unofficial agencies concerning injuries and deaths caused by opera-

[15] City Bank Farmers' Trust Co v. United States, 74 F.2d 692 (C.C.A. 2d 1935).

tion of automobiles on the highways of the country[16] was not judicially noticing or declaring that the statements and figures therein were precisely accurate. It was noticing that the injuries were in such great and increasing numbers as to cause public concern, and this, taken in connection with other almost universally known facts, formed a solid basis for the conclusion that the automobile driven on public highways was in fact a dangerous instrumentality and should be so classified as a matter of law. Professor Thayer's argument and illustrations, therefore, do not support his conclusion.

And Wigmore's text is no better. His citations are of no value. The Mayes case not only does not support him, it is almost squarely contrary. The trial judge judicially noticed the time at which the moon rose on the night at the place in question, and instructed the jury accordingly. The appellate court refused to consider affidavits tending to show that the judge was mistaken. The basis of the decision was that a judicially noticed matter does not depend upon the weight of evidence and is not to be determined upon a consideration of the credibility of witnesses, and that "the appellate court takes judicial notice of the fact in the same manner as does the trial court." The Kincaid decision contains nothing but an ambiguous dictum to justify its citation. Upon the issue whether the town of Gold Hill had a population of less than 500 in 1929, the court first took judicial notice that the population in 1920 as shown by the census was 442, and that this certainly did not preclude defendant from showing it to be over

[16] Southern Cotton Oil Company v. Anderson, 80 Fla. 441, 86 So. 629 (1920).

500 in 1929. Although the evidence offered by the defendant was inadmissible as hearsay, still the prosecution had the burden of showing that the population in 1929 was under 500, and it failed to do so because a showing that the population was 442 in 1920 was insufficient in the light of judicially known facts as to the normal growth of population. The citation of the case can be explained only because the court in pointing out that the defendant could have offered direct nonhearsay testimony as to the population in 1929 said: "Judicial notice would not preclude him from establishing the truth."

There can be little or no doubt that the weight of judicial authority rejects evidence as to matters properly subject to judicial notice. It is difficult to find cases decided before 1900 which even question this proposition, but the great and well deserved reputation of Wigmore has caused the quotation and citation of his statement to be made in a goodly number of later judicial opinions. It is believed that in all of these the citation is inapt or is explainable on other grounds—that the matter as to which the evidence was offered was either clearly without the realm of judicial notice or fell within that group of situations where the indisputability of the matter was itself disputable.

In *Timson v. Manufactured Coal & Coke Co.*,[17] the majority of the Supreme Court of Missouri, citing Wigmore, said:

> Judicially noticing facts, like many presumptions entertained by the courts, is but a rule of evidence; and, if the question is a disputable one, or can be disputed, evidence so disputing it is competent and should be admitted.

[17] 220 Mo. 580, 598, 119 S.W. 565, 569 (1909).

The question was whether a particular coal mine generated gas; the trial judge had taken judicial notice that it did generate gas because he thought it indisputable that all coal mines in Missouri generated gas. The majority of the Supreme Court held this charge incorrect. The Chief Justice dissented on the ground that the Court must know that this mine, operated as the evidence showed it was being operated, did generate gas. The subject of disagreement, therefore, was clearly whether the matter fell within the field of judicial notice. The question as to admissibility of evidence was said by the majority to depend upon whether the matter was disputable or could be disputed. That is not the Wigmore doctrine. Hence the citation is inapplicable.

In a small group of recent decisions the statement of Wigmore is quoted or referred to, but in most of them it was of no controlling importance. In a Maryland case [18] the issue was whether the court could on demurrer disregard an allegation that a proposed structure, if built over a specified portion of a highway, would not interfere with a special interest in the highway of owners of other property abutting on the highway. The court held the doctrine of judicial notice not applicable. In Appeal of Albert,[19] the Supreme Court of Pennsylvania pointed out the absurdity of submitting to successive juries a matter notoriously not subject to dispute; stated that perhaps the "presumption" created by judicial notice is not conclusive, but held that if Wigmore's assertions were accepted, still the

[18] Macht v. Hecht Co., 191 Md. 98, 59 A.2d 754 (1948).

[19] Appeal of Albert, 372 Pa. 13, 92 A.2d 663 (1952).

complaining party could not rely upon them because of her failure to take the necessary action in the court below. In a Utah case [20] the majority of the court made extensive quotations from Wigmore to support the reversal of a conviction in which the judge judicially noticed that in 1950 or 1951 a 1947 Ford sedan in excellent condition was worth more than $50.00, and consequently charged the jury that if they found defendant guilty of stealing it, they must find him guilty of grand larceny. The real ground of decision was that a court had no power to direct a jury to find against a defendant a necessary element of an offense since it had no power to direct a verdict of guilty. The Chief Justice dissented in a forceful opinion.

Two of our most respected and most learned jurists, Judge Learned Hand and the late Mr. Justice Cardozo, have likewise given unnecessary approval to Wigmore's dictum. In the Aluminum Co. case [21] Judge Hand, in holding that the appellate court would not accept as conclusive assertions in the report of a congressional committee made after the trial of the case, concerning the amount of bauxite in Arkansas, thought it appropriate to cite Wigmore. To have treated as indisputable a statement of fact which could not possibly have been within the personal knowledge of the members of the committee would have violated all legal precedent as well as every tenet of common sense. The court did, and probably rightly, take notice of the existence and content of the report, and considered it as a source of evidence sufficiently reliable to justify remand-

[20] State v. Lawrence, 234 P.2d 600 (1951).

[21] United States v. Aluminum Co. of America, 148 F.2d 416, 446 (2d Cir. 1945).

ing the case for further hearing. For such a ruling the reference to Wigmore was needless, if not entirely irrelevant. Mr. Justice Cardozo's citation was in the course of his opinion in the Ohio Bell Telephone case.[22] There the decision against the company was sought to be upheld by reliance "upon the strength of information recently collected and never yet disclosed" to the company, of which it was claimed the Public Utilities Commission of Ohio properly took official or judicial notice. The information was contained in documents which the commission had refused to allow the company to examine or analyze, information which the company was given no opportunity to explain or rebut. Certainly the Wigmore doctrine had no application to such a situation. All that was decided, and all that was needed was a decision that a party could not ask that a finding be upheld by reliance upon assertions made in documents brought to the attention of the trial tribunal after the close of the trial without giving the party against whom they were to be used an opportunity to know the content of the documents or to demonstrate to the tribunal that the assertions did not fall within the field of judicial notice.

Thayer does not attempt to explain any of the decisions rejecting evidence to support or contradict the matter judicially noticed. Both he and Wigmore would agree that evidence in support of it would be unnecessary. No doubt both would agree also that evidence as to the tenor of a rule of domestic law should not be received, for certainly

[22] Ohio Bell Tel. Co. v. Public Utilities Comm. of Ohio, 301 U.S. 292, 300 (1937).

that cannot be determined one way at one time and another at another time according to the weight of the evidence as it happens to be presented in the case at bar. What of official acts of the domestic government such as the recognition of a foreign government by the United States or the existence of a state of war or insurrection? Wigmore suggests that the former is a question "whether as a matter of substantive law and judicial functions a foreign State or Government will in domestic courts be treated as existing only so far as the Executive so treats it." [23] Let that be granted. The decision of the Executive is final as a matter of substantive law, but that does not signify whether or not a particular foreign government has been recognized by the Executive. That is a question of fact, and the proposition of fact is indisputable and is easily ascertained by resort to available sources of indisputable accuracy. It is not within the realm of the disputable and is not to be determined by evidence. Much the same is true as to the existence of a state of war or insurrection. Insofar as the action of the political department is conclusive, the question of what, if any, action has been taken by that department, is a question of fact. It is subject to judicial notice. Consequently the Supreme Court of Kansas knew what it was talking about and meant what it said when it declared that it took judicial notice that after the acquisition of the Philippines in 1898 until later than 1902 the island of Mindanao was in a state of insurrection amounting to war, that the matter thus noticed was learned by consultation of official documents of the Executive Department, that

[23] 9 WIGMORE, EVIDENCE §2566(3) (3d ed. 1940).

it was indisputable, and that evidence to prove the contrary was inadmissible.[24] Nor can this decision be explained away as laying down a rule of substantive law only. And the same is obviously true of other cases rejecting evidence. The Supreme Court of Errors of Connecticut was not creating a rule of law when it held that the court must instruct the jury that June 3, 1906, fell on Sunday,[25] although there was conflicting evidence from which the contrary might have been found, nor was it merely deciding upon the proper allocation of function between judge and jury. Neither was the California court doing so when it determined the time that the moon rose in a specified place on a specified date. And no one could reasonably argue that the Supreme Court of New Jersey was laying down a rule of domestic law when by its own examination of New York decisions it determined that the law of New York was contrary to that testified to by experts at the trial.[26]

It is submitted (1) that an examination of the authorities will reveal a number of decisions rejecting or disregarding evidence tending to prove the contrary of a judicially noticed matter that can be explained on no other ground than that the matter is indisputable; (2) that almost, if not quite all the cases enunciating the Thayer-Wigmore doctrine can be explained on the ground that the matter in question was disputable, or in an exceptional situation such as that in the Utah case that the trier of fact had the legal

[24] La Rue v. Kansas Mutual Life Ins. Co., 68 Kan. 539, 75 Pac. 494 (1904).

[25] Beardsley v. Irving, 81 Conn. 489, 71 Atl. 580 (1909).

[26] State v. Cromwell, 6 N.J. Misc. 221, 140 Atl. 429 (Sup. Ct. 1928).

power to disregard the indisputable in favor of a defendant in a criminal case; (3) that no case can be found in which a judge was reversed for rejecting evidence tending to prove the contrary of a matter properly within the realm of judicial notice. The decisions rejecting such evidence cannot be harmonized with the Wigmore doctrine, which in effect is that there is no matter of fact not subject to dispute in litigation. If Thayer's "cannot well be supposed to admit of contradiction" means that the matters mentioned are not subject to dispute in litigation, he in effect recognizes two classes: (1) facts noticed as conclusively indisputable, and (2) facts noticed as *prima facie* indisputable.

It will be observed that Thayer says that "taking judicial notice of a fact is merely presuming it." Wigmore uses the language of assumption—the court assumes that the matter will not be disputed. They both emphasize the use of judicial notice as a device for expediting the trial. This puts it in the same category with rules fixing the burden of producing evidence and the burden of persuasion. Indeed, their treatment of the doctrine seems to make it a species of presumption, and the Supreme Court of Pennsylvania in dealing with Wigmore's view put it in terms of presumptions.

Practitioners can be thankful that the courts have not as yet beclouded the law of judicial notice by treating it as a part of the law of presumptions. Thayer does not even mention it in his essay on "Presumptions," though he speaks of a presumption and of judicial notice, each in its place, as a *prima facie* assumption. And it is to be fervently hoped that the courts will never enmesh the problems of judicial notice in the language of presumptions. Thayer in 1898 began his discussion of presumptions with a quotation from Alciatus,[27] written some three hundred years earlier, to the effect that the subject was even then in almost inextricable confusion. And Thayer's attempt "to relieve the subject of much of its obscurity" has not been highly successful, for the American cases exhibit at least eight different views of which that advocated by Thayer is only one. Incidentally, the American Law Institute's original acceptance of the Thayer view was not adopted by the Uniform Commissioners, and Wigmore was constrained in his third edition to propose that the problem in litigation be handled by a rather elaborate and somewhat complicated procedure, involving a pretrial or interlocutory hearing and the submission of special questions to the jury.

Even if the language of presumptions is avoided and it is said merely that judicially noticed matter is subject to rebuttal, members of the trial bar will soon be demanding that the judge declare the exact effect of judicial notice. It is the universally accepted doctrine that the judge in determining the tenor of the matter judicially noticed is free to consult all sources of information that he deems worth while. Is this to be abandoned? If not, must each and every source examined be disclosed to counsel, and, if disclosed, is the author of any cited statement to be subject to subpoena and cross-examination? Is the judge to be subject to a cross-examination as to the extent of his reliance

[27] THAYER, A PRELIMINARY TREATISE ON EVIDENCE AT THE COMMON LAW 313 (1898).

upon each item of information that he has gathered and as to the validity of his deductions therefrom? How much evidence and of what quality is required to make the judicially known matter a question for the trier of fact? What effect does the taking of judicial notice have on the burden of persuasion as distinguished from the burden of producing evidence? In a trial by jury what, if anything, is the judge to tell the jury about the judicially noticed matter? If rebuttable judicial notice is not a synonym for presumption, just how does it differ from a presumption?

The problem is not one of terminology. It is not one of defining the limits of the field of judicial notice, for the Wigmore doctrine in theory denies the legal indisputability of any proposition of fact, although no judicial decision has ever gone so far. Rather, it is, I contend, as I have previously stated in summary: [28]

". . . . If the field of judicial notice of facts contains only the indisputable, then the path of counsel is clear. The party seeking judicial notice has the burden of convincing the judge that (*a*) the matter is so notorious as not to be the subject of dispute among reasonable men or (*b*) the matter is capable of immediate accurate demonstration by resort to readily accessible sources of indisputable accuracy. There is no artificial limit upon the sources of information which he may furnish the judge, and none upon those which the judge may consult of his own motion. The opponent likewise is not restricted by rules of evidence in offering, or inducing the judge to consult reliable repositories of relevant data. If the judge believes it doubtful

[28] Morgan, *Judicial Notice*, 57 HARV. L. REV. 269, 286–87 (1944).

whether the matter falls within the domain of judicial notice, or if the sources available are inadequate, he leaves the subject within the domain of evidence, and all the ordinary rules applicable to the process of resolving an ordinary issue of fact are enforced. If he is convinced that the matter is within the field of judicial notice and of the tenor of the matter to be noticed, he removes it from the field of dispute. If the field of judicial notice contains both the disputable and the indisputable, where is the line drawn? What guide can counsel or a trial judge use? When do the rules of evidence come into operation, and when are the ordinary criteria for directing a nonsuit or a verdict or finding applicable? If all matters within the field are disputable, then all possible questions as to the exact function of judicial notice and its relation to presumptions will demand answers. It is submitted that not only theoretical symmetry but also practical considerations strongly support the thesis that matter in the field of judicial notice is not subject to attack by evidence. If there be a dispute as to whether a matter is a subject of dispute, the question to be answered is whether the matter lies within the field of evidence or within the field of judicial notice; and the material which may be presented or consulted in a search for the answer is in no respect limited by the rules of evidence."

III

If the foregoing analysis is accepted, it must follow that Thayer is right in declaring the doctrine applicable,

> Wherever the process of reasoning has a place, and that is everywhere. Not peculiarly in the law of evidence. It does, indeed,

find in the region of evidence a frequent and conspicuous application; but the habit of regarding this topic as a mere title in the law of evidence obscures the true conception of both subjects.[29]

Wigmore disagrees; he would confine the topic to the field of evidence, and give other explanations of other situations in which the language of judicial notice is used. This means, of course, that he would not classify matters of domestic law as within the scope of judicial notice, for no one doubts that the courts at every stage of a lawsuit must know and apply the law of the forum. Thayer accepts the word of the courts when they declare that they are taking judicial notice of specified matters, for example, in passing upon the sufficiency of a pleading, or in interpreting a statute or other writing, or in modifying a rule of the common law by making it applicable to a new situation, or in determining the validity or constitutionality of legislation. Wigmore's explanation of the result in these four situations does not question the propriety of accepting as true, without requiring evidence, what the court deems indisputable. Does his explanation serve any useful purpose?

1. The earliest reports contain precedents of reliance upon judicial notice in dealing with pleadings. In 1635 the court held of no effect an allegation in defendant's plea that he had thrown stones at plaintiff gently and with a gentle hand.[30]

2. A Georgia court held that an allegation in a complaint for wrongful death, that the deceased child aged one year,

[29] Thayer, *op. cit.*, note 27, 278 (1898).
[30] Cole v. Maunder, 2 Roll. Abr. 548 (1635).

eight months and ten days had rendered services to its parents of the value of $2.00 per month in picking up chips and amusing the baby, was contrary to what the court judicially knew, namely, that a child of that age was incapable of rendering services of pecuniary value.[31] This, of course, may be explained as a construction of the Georgia statute—a matter of substantive law, as Wigmore suggests. But that does not avoid the truth that the court was judicially noticing the truth of a proposition of generalized knowledge in construing words the ordinary meaning of which it also judicially knew. And how does it change the nature of the process that a statute rather than a common-law rule was involved or that the problem arose on demurrer rather than on an offer of evidence? California and Tennessee cases have applied the same rule to allegations contrary to legislative records of indisputable accuracy accessible to the court.[32]

Rules of procedure governing pleadings may render judicial knowledge immaterial, but they do not destroy the court's power or duty to take judicial notice. For example the New York courts in 1815 certainly had judicial knowledge of the existence of a state of war between Great Britain and the United States in July, 1812, but an allegation that a shipment of goods was made between Liverpool and New Orleans during that month was held not to be an allegation that it was made in time of war. The common-law rule required that a pleader must state the time of every material fact alleged but that except where the time

[31] Southern Railway Co. v. Covenia, 100 Ga. 46, 29 S.E. 219 (1896).

[32] French v. Senate, 146 Cal. 604, 80 Pac. 1031 (1905); Heiskell v. Knox County, 132 Tenn. 180, 177 S.W. 483 (1915).

was of the essence of the cause, no issue could be taken upon the allegation of time.[33] For a similar reason an early English case held that an allegation that a killing occurred between the hours of five and six in November was not an allegation that it occurred in the nighttime.[34]

3. It is the boast of common lawyers that the law is molded to meet changing conditions. The knowledge of the changed conditions comes to the court not by the presentation of evidence but through judicial notice. In developing the law of torts, both as applied to relations between master and servant and as applied to personal and vicarious responsibility in general, the courts framed and reframed the rules as they took judicial knowledge of the dangers involved in the handling and use of poisons, explosives, and power-driven machinery. So in determining to what extent common-law concepts should be retained or modified as to the use of the air space above real property, they need no evidence as to the existence of the airplane or of the dangers involved in its ordinary operation or of its constantly increasing use as a means of transportation. The various doctrines of vicarious responsibility of the owner of an automobile have been based on what the courts judicially know of the dangers to which it has exposed the public when driven upon the highways of the country.

4. When the constitutionality of a statute is attacked the courts consciously and consistently make use of the doctrine, and frequently so declare. Indeed, there was a

[33] Amory v. M'Gregor, 12 Johns. (N.Y.) 287 (1815).
[34] Mackelley's Case, 1 Roll. Abr. 524 (1612).

time, not too distant, when they seemed to think that judicial notice was the sole source of information as to relevant propositions of generalized knowledge and as to all pertinent details in the general factual situation to which the statute would apply or was intended to apply. Recently the appellate courts have come to recognize that many relevant matters, even if indisputable, or within the judicial knowledge of the trial court, may be unknown actually and judicially to them, and they have required that the necessary information be included in the appellate record. This is merely applying to the question of constitutionality a rule that has long been applicable in other situations. Before an appellate court can intelligently pass upon the validity of the action of a lower court, it must have all relevant data before it. And in most situations, it must put upon one party or the other the burden of supplying those data in the record. When they are not supplied, the only problem is whether the court shall require the data to be then and there supplied, or whether it shall remand the case to have the record corrected, or shall make its decision on the assumption that the missing data are adverse to the contention of the party who failed to see that they were in the record. Insofar as this affects judicial notice, it does no more than require a party to present the judicially noticed material in an appropriate manner.

5. Incidentally, the same process is employed in ruling on objections to evidence as irrelevant. Michael and Adler have demonstrated that in ruling upon an objection to an item of circumstantial evidence on the ground of irrelevancy, the judge must constantly rely upon judicially known

propositions of generalized knowledge. If evidence of fact A is offered as tending to prove fact D and the line of reasoning is that from A, B may be inferred; from B, C may be inferred; and from C, D, no single step can be taken unless the specified fact is conjoined with a proposition of generalized knowledge whether or not articulated. Wigmore would doubtless agree, but he would object to dealing with this process in terms of judicial notice rather than merely as a part of the process of reasoning.

My submission, therefore, is that Thayer's view is to be preferred to Wigmore's. Resort to the basic reason for judicial notice determines not only the limits of the matter noticed but also the extent of the field of its application in litigation. There is no part of the judicial process in which the court may properly disregard what is so widely accepted as true as not to be subject of reasonable dispute or what can be immediately and accurately demonstrated to be true by resort to easily accessible sources of indisputable accuracy.

## IV

Judicial notice may be a dangerous device in the hands of a judge who is opinionated or conceited or who inadvertently assumes the nonexistence of pertinent data. The Ohio Bell Telephone case indicates the possibilities of its abuse or misuse before a tribunal which may misunderstand it or may think itself entitled to act *ex parte*. Generally speaking, the judicial decisions do not show an appreciation of these dangers or indeed a realization of the harm that may be done by assuming the indisputability of the disputable or the accuracy of a source of information which may be open to question. Indeed, some courts of last resort have, or seem to have, assumed that knowledge of the segment of human experience known to their respective judges constitutes all that can be known about human experience in general. There are decisions of the United States Supreme Court declaring unconstitutional legislation designed to change long accepted legal concepts because the Court or a majority of its members deemed to be incontrovertibly true what many informed people and some later courts believed to be demonstrably false. In such a situation there is often no opportunity for the parties or their counsel to be heard on the question whether the subject matter is within the domain of judicial notice or the proposition deemed incontestably true is accurately phrased. Litigants should not be exposed to these risks. For this reason both the American Law Institute and the proposed Uniform Rules of Evidence set up safeguards against them (*a*) by requiring that the party requesting judicial notice furnish the judge sufficient information and give each adverse party notice necessary to enable him to meet the request; (*b*) by providing that the judge shall decline to take judicial notice of a matter unless it clearly is indisputable; (*c*) by directing the judge, where the fact would in the absence of judicial notice be determined by the trier of fact, to direct the jury to find the matter as judicially noticed, or, in a nonjury case, to include in the record of the trial a statement of the matter so noticed; (*d*) by making it mandatory that the judge inform the parties of the tenor of any matter to be judicially noticed by him and afford each of them reasonable opportunity to present to him information relevant to the propriety of taking such judicial notice or to the tenor of the matter to be noticed; and (*e*) by allowing both the trial judge in proceedings subsequent to trial and the reviewing court to take judicial notice, but requiring in such event that the parties be afforded reasonable opportunity to present information relevant to the propriety of taking such judicial notice and to the tenor of the matter to be noticed.

With such guaranties against abuse courts may, to the great benefit of the public and of litigants, be liberal in the use of judicial notice. They may greatly expedite trials by judicially noticing facts which are contemporaneously so notoriously true as to be incontrovertible in the community, even though these facts may not remain so for any considerable time thereafter. They may profitably make much more frequent resort to available sources of indisputable accuracy. Pretrial proceedings offer peculiar opportunities for a judicious application of judicial notice. Its employment under proper safeguards at every stage of the judicial process will greatly further the accomplishment of a chief objective of all sound procedure: the elimination of issues as to which there is or can be no bona fide dispute.

# FUNCTIONS OF JUDGE AND JURY

DISCUSSIONS OF this subject are usually confined to an examination of the respective functions of judge and jury concerning issues of fact upon the resolution of which the admissibility of offered evidence depends. There is seldom, if ever, any mention of the extent to which the judge does and should decide questions of fact by allocating the burden of proof and giving binding instructions as to the requisites for its discharge. This seems to me well worth serious consideration for the courts regard this burden as so important as to consider it for many purposes a matter of substance rather than procedure, and an error in allocating it to be ground for reversal. Therefore, I shall treat of this topic first. Thereafter, I shall examine some typical authorities dealing with the function of the judge in ruling on the admissibility of evidence, with a view to discovering what principle is or should be controlling.

## I. ALLOCATING AND DISCHARGING THE BURDEN OF PROOF

*Introduction—the Two Burdens* I begin by reminding you that when the trier of fact is unable to determine the truth or falsity of a disputed proposition of fact, he must render his decision against the party having the burden of proof. Consequently, in a jury trial the judge by allocating the burden of proof decides each issue of fact which the jury is unable to decide. This rests upon the questionable assumption that the jury understands and follows the directions of the judge concerning both the incidence of the burden and the state of mind of each juror required for a finding by him that the burden has been discharged. However high or low an opinion we may have as to the efficacy of the usual charge to enlighten or control the jury, I submit (*a*) that the courts in determining which party must bear this burden should have clearly in mind the consequences of the decision and should be guided by reasons of substance and policy; no mere dogma should be given the slightest consideration, no matter how high its source or how often it has been repeated; and (*b*) that the guide given to the jury for the exercise of its judgment in dealing with the evidence should be stated in language intelligible to the judge who uses it, to the jurors who must apply it, and to the appellate justices who review it. Let me first state a few obvious but fundamental propositions:

1. Under our adversary system the judge judicially knows all the rules of law applicable to any justiciable controversy that may be presented to the court. He knows nothing about the existence of a controversy until it is properly initiated by the parties. As to the truth, falsity, or probability of any disputable proposition of fact presented for decision, the judge knows nothing. Neither he nor the court of which he is a part has any machinery for investigation. The trial, as Michael and Adler have shown,[1] is not an investigative,

[1] See Michael and Adler, *Real Proof,* 5 VAND. L. REV. 344 (1952), and references there given to other discussions by the same authors.

but a demonstrative proceeding. It is the function of the parties to supply the information which is the basis for the persuasion of the jury.

2. Each proposition of fact which makes an issue for trial is phrased in terms of certainty. It asserts that an event did or did not occur or that a condition did or does exist or did not or does not exist. Suppose that plaintiff's proposition is that event X occurred and defendant's that X did not occur. Although neither judge nor jury has any information as to the facts, the court does not assume the likelihood of the occurrence of X and that of its nonoccurrence to be equal. It assumes either that X did or did not occur. If it assumes that X did not occur, plaintiff will lose unless information is furnished, that is, speaking generally, unless evidence is introduced which (*a*) is sufficient to justify a reasonable jury in finding that X did occur and (*b*) persuades the particular jury to find that X did occur. For the verdict of the jury, like the allegations of the pleadings, speaks in terms of certainty. In such a situation, it is usually said that plaintiff has two burdens, the burden of producing or going forward with evidence and the burden of persuasion. More accurately stated, plaintiff bears two risks, the risk of nonproduction and the risk of nonpersuasion, for the party with the burden merely carries the risk that the evidence may not be introduced or that the jury may not be persuaded. The evidence or argument or both by which each burden is lifted may be furnished by the opponent.

The burden or risk of producing the evidence requisite to get to the jury, is often called the burden of evidence, and the other, the burden of persuasion. With the burden of evidence the jury has nothing to do. The judge alone decides which party must bear it and whether it has been lifted. If at the close of the evidence he has determined that it has been lifted, the jury alone deals with the other burden. It is the jury that has to be persuaded.

3. The allocation of the burden of evidence as to each issue in the case must be first fixed at or before the beginning of the trial. This is of high importance to the parties, for a party is not permitted to put in his evidence piecemeal. If he bears this burden as to the occurrence of X, he must introduce all his available evidence that X did occur. He may not introduce just enough to justify a finding in his favor and reserve the remainder for a later stage of the trial. Furthermore, a plaintiff's right to close to the jury depended at common law—and under modern procedure may still depend—upon his bearing this burden at the opening of the trial as to any matter essential to entitle him to the relief he is seeking. If plaintiff begins with this burden, defendant may require the judge at the close of plaintiff's evidence to determine whether the burden has been lifted; and at the close of defendant's evidence, plaintiff may require a ruling whether the burden then rests upon defendant. At the close of all the evidence, either party may by a motion for a directed verdict secure a decision whether the burden then rests upon his opponent. The allocation of the burden of persuasion becomes of importance only after the burden of evidence no longer rests on either party and the evidence has been closed. For only then need the judge rule upon the burden of persuasion, and be prepared to charge

the jury concerning it. Only then do the parties need to know of it so that counsel can effectively frame their summation arguments.

4. To persuade the jury means to persuade every member of the jury. If a juror understands just what proposition of fact he must be persuaded is true in order to be persuaded to find that X occurred, and if he is persuaded that it is true, he finds for plaintiff; if he is persuaded that it is false, he finds for defendant. If he is persuaded either way, it is entirely immaterial which party has had the burden. It is only when he is persuaded that the truth of a proposition and its falsity are equally likely, when his mind is in equilibrium, that the incidence of the burden is important and then it is decisive. Then he must find the proposition false. No juror can refuse to make a decision because he deems the data presented inadequate. To fail to find for the party having the burden is to find against him. If some of the jurors are persuaded that the proposition is false and the mind of each of the others is in equilibrium, the verdict must be that the proposition is false. If a single juror is persuaded that the proposition is true and the others are not so persuaded, there can be no verdict; the result is a mistrial.

*Allocating the Burdens—Effect of Presumptions* Before Thayer wrote, there was little judicially expressed appreciation of the distinction between the two burdens. The term "burden of proof" was used to designate either or both. There was little reason to discriminate, for it was, or seemed to be, assumed that the two burdens were coincident, and in numerous situations to have made the distinction would have served no purpose. Consequently there was little discussion of reasons for fixing the burden of evidence. The judicial opinions, however, are replete with suggested formulae for fixing the burden of proof. They almost always concern the burden of persuasion. On analysis most of them have little practical value. Five of them merit comment:

1. The burden is upon the party asserting the affirmative of the issue. No court now accepts this without explaining that the affirmative of an issue may include or consist of a negative.

2. In insisting that the confusion in the authorities was due to the application of a verbal instead of a legal affirmative, the renowned Mr. Justice Doe said that a "plain principle of natural justice" requires a party to prove the essential facts of his case "whether he states them in the form of a negative affirmation or in any other form." But he gave no a priori test for determining when a verbal negative is a legal affirmative or whether a particular fact is essential to the case of one party rather than the other.

3. The burden of persuasion is coincident with the burden of pleading. This is helpful at best only where available precedents establish the pleading rule. And these burdens were not coincident at common law in actions in which the general issue was given wide scope; they are not always coincident under the typical code; and in modern procedure, where the pleadings are cut off with the answer, many issues not revealed by the pleadings must be tried.

4. A party who has peculiar knowledge of a fact or peculiar means of access to evidence of its existence has the burden of making it known. This seems reasonable enough,

but reasons of policy often outweigh this one reason of convenience.

5. The truth is, and the commentators and modern judges say so in plain language, that "where the burden of proof should rest is merely a question of policy and fairness based on experience in the different situations." [2]

Considerations of fairness and policy based on experience should be quite as effective in determining the allocation of the burden of evidence as in determining the allocation of the burden of persuasion. Mere procedural convenience may well be controlling as to the burden of evidence and still be of slight consequence as to the burden of persuasion. For example, the Supreme Court of the United States has made its concept of the demands of social policy fix upon the prosecution in a federal court the burden of persuading the jury beyond reasonable doubt that the defendant was sane at the time of the offense charged. There is, however, a presumption, which the court recognizes, that the defendant was sane. This justifies requiring the defendant to demonstrate that his claim of irresponsibility has some basis in fact as well as in statement. When once this appears, the effect of the presumption is dissipated, and the social policy fixing the burden of persuasion becomes effective. Many courts think that the demands of social policy fix upon the defendant not only the first burden but also the second.

Where a presumption comes into operation during the course of the trial, its effect is always at least to fix the burden of evidence upon the party who is denying the exist-

[2] Rustad v. Great Northern Ry. Co., 122 Minn. 453, 142 N.W. 727 (1913), opinion by Dibell, J.

ence of the presumed fact. Suppose a presumption that when the existence of fact M is established in an action, the existence of fact X is presumed. If the existence of M is established, the trier of fact must find that X exists unless and until evidence is introduced which would justify a finding of the nonexistence of X. Whether the compulsion should continue longer—until the evidence is believed by the trier or until the trier is persuaded to find the nonexistence of X or is convinced that its nonexistence and its existence are equally probable—should be determined by considerations of fairness and policy. The cases are in hopeless conflict, but the present tendency is to accept the doctrine, invented by Thayer and approved by Wigmore, that the sole function of every presumption is to fix the burden of evidence. Under this view the mere introduction of evidence which, if believed, would warrant a finding of the nonexistence of X destroys the presumption. It is immaterial whether or not the trier disbelieves the evidence and whether or not, if believed, it has any effect upon the trier's decision of the issue.

It was impossible for Thayer to ignore the universally accepted judicial opinion that certain presumptions can be overcome only by evidence having more than ordinary persuasive force. These he explained thus:

But in these cases, also, the presumption, merely as such, goes no further than to call for proof of that which it negatives; *i.e.*, for something which renders it probable. It does not specify how much; whether proof beyond a reasonable doubt or by a preponderance of all the evidence, or by any other measure of proof. From the nature of the case, in negativing a given supposition and calling for argument or evidence in support of it, there is meant such an amount of evidence or reason as may render the view contended for rationally probable. But beyond that, a presumption seems to say nothing. When, therefore, we read that the contrary of any particular presumption must be proved beyond a reasonable doubt, as is sometimes said, *e.g.*, of the "presumption of innocence" and the presumption of legitimacy, it is to be recognized that we have something superadded to the rule of presumption, namely, another rule as to the amount of evidence which is needed to overcome the presumption, or, in other words, to start the case of the party who is silenced by it. And so whenever any specific result is attributed to a presumption other than that of fixing the duty of going forward with proof. This last, and this alone, appears to be [the] characteristic and essential work of the presumption. It is the substantive criminal law and the substantive law as to persons respectively that fix the rule about the strength of conviction that must be produced in the mind of the tribunal in order to hold one guilty of crime, or to find a child born in wedlock to be illegitimate.[3]

What this seems to me to mean is: (1) everything which a court properly calls a presumption fixes the burden of producing evidence sufficient to justify a trier in finding the nonexistence of the presumed fact; (2) the presumption does nothing more, but it may be accompanied by a rule which prescribes the production of a quantity and quality of evidence sufficient to justify a finding beyond reasonable doubt that the presumed fact does not exist, but which says nothing concerning the effect which this evidence must have upon the mind of the trier; and (3) the substantive law applicable to the subject matter involved will determine the allocation of the burden of persuasion.

[3] THAYER, PRELIMINARY TREATISE ON EVIDENCE 313, 336–337 (1898).

If I am right, it all reduces to this: insofar as anything called a presumption is held by the courts to do something beyond requiring the production of evidence making a finding of the nonexistence of the presumed fact rationally probable, it is not the presumption which has this effect but the unspecified thing or things accompanying the presumption. If so, whenever during the course of a trial facts are established which bring a presumption into play, we must be free to inquire whether the presumption is accompanied by another rule and we should likewise be free to ask whether in this situation the applicable substantive law fixes the burden of persuasion at the same time that the presumption fixes the burden of producing evidence. And if this in turn is so, then Thayer has told us only that a court should never use the term presumption to describe a mere justifiable inference on the one hand or an irrebuttable proposition on the other, but only a compulsory tentative assumption, and that this accurate use of the term does not negative the existence of an accompanying unspecified, unarticulated rule regulating the burden and measure of persuasion. And this means only that we have been given a warning against the loose use of language and the need for an accurate terminology. But it must be admitted that Thayer's disciples will not concede that his doctrine does not carry such a negation.

When the courts were confusing the two burdens and assuming them to be coincident, the burden of persuasion as to each material proposition expressly asserted and denied in the pleadings was necessarily fixed at the commencement of the trial; and as to any other disputed material proposition first revealed during the trial, it was fixed as it would have been fixed if the issue had been made in the pleadings. Acceptance of Thayer's doctrine as to the effect of a presumption goes far toward compelling acceptance of his related conclusion that the burden of persuasion, once fixed, never shifts. His discussion implies that when the issue is not made by the pleadings, the disputed proposition should be formulated in the terms of a properly pleaded allegation of fact—an allegation of so-called ultimate fact. It disregards three important considerations: (1) the allocation of the burden of persuasion, as distinguished from the burden of producing evidence, has no legal significance until the case is in the hands of the jury; (2) the judge need not decide which party must bear it until he formulates his charge after the close of the evidence; and (3) knowledge of the judge's decision upon this matter is of slight importance to counsel until preparation of his final argument. These make groundless the accepted notion that the incidence of the burden should depend upon the situation as it appears at the commencement of the action. If considerations of policy and fairness are to be controlling in determining which party should bear the burden, those pertinent at the close of the evidence to the situation with which the jury has to deal should be applicable, and the burden should be fixed as of that time. Then no question of shifting could arise. The rules which Thayer described as accompanying the presumption and the substantive rules of policy as to burden of persuasion involved could then be applied without requiring fantastic mental gymnastics to support the proposition that the burden of persuasion had not shifted in cases where it lay on the plaintiff at the commencement of the action and on the defendant at the close of the evidence, as in the Vermont case of Jones' Estate where plaintiff began with the burden of proving himself the legitimate child of Henry and defendant at the end had to persuade the jury beyond reasonable doubt that plaintiff was not the child of Henry.[4] Of course, sensible procedure would require the abandonment of the Thayer doctrine as to presumptions and concede that the establishment of facts which create a presumption does in some situations and should in most cases fix the burden of persuasion as Rule 14 of the Uniform Rules of Evidence provides. Just as the courts have come to recognize that there is no a priori formula for fixing the burden of persuasion, so they should recognize that if there is a good reason for putting on one party or the other the burden of going forward with evidence—if it might not as well have been determined by chance—it ought to be good enough to control a finding when the mind of the trier is in equilibrium.

*Charging on the Burden of Persuasion* When at the close of the evidence the judge has decided that the burden of producing evidence lies on neither party, he is faced with the problem of communicating to the jury a guide for their deliberations. No lawyer need be told of the inadequacies of words as a means of communicating legal concepts to laymen, but all will agree with Judge Jerome Frank:

[4] 110 Vt. 438, 8 A.2d 631 (1939). See criticism in note 21, p. 98, of MORGAN AND MAGUIRE, CASES AND MATERIALS ON EVIDENCE (3d ed. 1951).

But no matter what the difficulties may be of rendering many of the legal rules intelligible to the jury, surely the most important part of the judge's charge relative to the facts—i.e., that of dealing with the burden of proof—ought to be so worded that the jurors can comprehend it.[5]

Does the charge as usually given meet this minimum standard? The opinions which discuss the form of words to be used are legion. The opinion of Mr. Justice Schenck of the Supreme Court of North Carolina will serve as an example:

In this jurisdiction there are three degrees of proof required of the party upon whom the *onus probandi* rests. First, in ordinary civil actions the burden is to satisfy the jury by the greater weight of the evidence; and, second, in certain cases of an equitable nature, such as where it is sought to reform a written instrument, or prove the terms of a lost will, or to impeach the probate of a married woman's deed, the burden is to establish the contention by clear, strong and cogent proof; and, third, in criminal actions the burden is to show the guilt of the accused beyond a reasonable doubt.[6]

[5] Larson v. Jo Ann Cab Corp., 209 F.2d 929, 935 (1954). Yet after having demonstrated the likelihood that the use of the usual language will mislead and that to speak of "a degree of conviction favorable to his contention" is still more likely to mislead, and after citing numerous nonlegal authorities to show the dangers in the use of ambiguous phrases, he upholds a charge which makes use of both phrases and multiplies the ambiguities, because it is on the whole no worse than the orthodox charge. He ends in effect with the counsel of despair that attempts to improve the orthodox charge should be postponed "until such time as we have satisfactory returns from checks of popular reactions to the traditional formulas."

[6] Williams v. Blue Ridge Building and Loan Ass'n, 207 N.C. 362, 177 S.E. 176 (1934).

He explained that in the second class the burden is to "satisfy fully" but not to "satisfy to a moral certainty," and that in using the latter phrase, the trial judge committed reversible error. Some courts condemn the use of "satisfy"; Alabama approves it only if it is qualified by the adverb "reasonably"; others prohibit any adjective qualifying "preponderance" in the phrase "preponderance of evidence." No trial judge can safely do other than use the form of words approved by the court of last resort of his jurisdiction.

The courts generally agree with the classification of Mr. Justice Schenck and with the description of the evidence required. Like him, they do not explain what they mean by "establish his contention" or any equivalent phrase. In the civil cases they emphasize the means of persuasion, the quantity and quality of the evidence; in the criminal case, it is the state of mind produced by the evidence that is made decisive. They generally point out that greater weight or preponderance does not refer to number of witnesses or quantity of evidence but to the convincing force of the evidence, and they sometimes use, and permit counsel to use, the simile of a pair of scales with the evidence of one party in one pan and that of the other party in the other. This may be, and often is, highly misleading because one party may produce evidence more convincing than that of the other, which will nevertheless be insufficient to support a finding.

In a few jurisdictions the courts have been forced to explain just what proposition the jury must find to be true if they are to find for the party having the burden. If a party has the burden of persuasion that event X occurred, in Connecticut and California the proposition is that it is more probable that X occurred than that X did not occur. In Wisconsin and Missouri, the proposition is that X did occur, and it is not enough that the jurors find its occurrence more probable than its nonoccurrence; if they can go no further than that, they must find its nonoccurrence. In Massachusetts Mr. Justice Lummus, speaking for the Supreme Judicial Court, has declared:

> After the evidence has been weighed, that proposition is proved by a preponderance of the evidence if it is made to appear more likely or probable in the sense that actual belief in its truth, derived from the evidence, exists in the mind or minds of the tribunal notwithstanding any doubts that may still linger there.[7]

In the light of these conflicting views, how can a jury be expected to know what is meant by the usual charge in the usual civil case? And in the cases of the second class, will not the average man think that any evidence that convinces him is satisfactory and convincing? Is not the idea intended to be conveyed one that has to do with the degree of likelihood which the jury must find? It is too clear for argument that it is impossible in a judicial proceeding to acquire accurate knowledge concerning a past event as to which there is a dispute. The most that can be expected is a demonstration of the preponderance of probability. If so, why not say so to the jurors in terms that any layman can understand: "Does the evidence convince you that it

[7] Sargent v. Massachusetts Accident Co., 307 Mass. 246, 29 N.E.2d 825, 827 (1940).

is more likely or probable that X occurred than that it did not occur?" Notwithstanding all the uncertainties and ambiguities in language, all the dangers that any word used by a speaker will mean one thing to him and another thing to his auditor, it is submitted that the meaning of such a question will be clear to any layman of sufficient intelligence to qualify as a juror. There is no need to talk of preponderance or weight of evidence. The question refers to all the evidence and asks an answer only as to its effect upon the juror's mind with reference to the truth of a clearly expressed proposition.

In a case of the second class, the idea to be conveyed can be expressed thus: "Does the evidence convince you that it is much more likely or probable that X occurred than that it did not occur?" In criminal cases experience has shown that the only part of the orthodox charge which has given trouble is the phrase "beyond reasonable doubt." Perhaps it may be wise to explain that it does not mean a possible or imaginary doubt, but the response of a Texas judge to an inquiry by a juror seems adequate: "I have a reasonable doubt whether any explanation I can give would make its meaning more clear to you." The mouth-filling phrase of Chief Justice Shaw, "an abiding conviction to a moral certainty of the truth of the charge," will not bear analysis. Suppose a juror asked him to define "moral certainty" or "abiding conviction" as distinguished from an amoral certainty, and to say how long a conviction must have or must have had an abode in his mind.

It is suggested that the orthodox charge with a simple statement that reasonable doubt means a doubt which a reasonable man would entertain and not a mere possibility of a doubt is a sufficient guide for the average juror. In civil cases, so long as the courts continue to use the orthodox phrasing, just so long will the concept conveyed to the jury be a matter of conjecture.

The truth is that in allocating the burden of persuasion and explaining to the jury their duties with reference to it, the courts have been performing their functions with a minimum of efficiency and with what President Eliot of Harvard once described as a maximum of intellectual frugality. It is high time that the entire subject be critically reexamined.

## II. RULING ON ADMISSIBILITY OF EVIDENCE

*Generally* That the incidence of the burden of persuasion is decisive when the mind of the trier is in equilibrium makes it crystal clear that the trial of an issue of fact is not a scientific investigation. It is a proceeding designed to secure by rational processes a factual basis for the orderly adjustment of a dispute between litigants, by a body of untrained triers who represent in theory a cross section of the community. It is also an adversary proceeding in which the litigants furnish almost all the materials, that is, the evidence and arguments, for decision as to the facts, and in which the triers are bound to use only the knowledge concerning the matter in dispute which they have acquired by what has occurred in their presence during the trial under the supervision of the judge. Consequently while the primary objective is a finding of fact in accord with the truth, the very nature of the proceeding and the character of the personnel involved impose limits upon the quantity and quality of the data available to the jury, limits which no one, layman or scientist, in search for the truth would tolerate. Because in theory the process is rational, Thayer's first proposition [8] is unquestioned, "that, without any exception, nothing which is not, or is not supposed to be, logically relevant is admissible." Because of the purpose of the proceeding, its adversary character, and the quality of the tribunal, his second proposition is accepted by the courts in principle, if not in statement, "that, subject to many exceptions and qualifications, whatever is logically relevant is admissible."

In the conduct of the trial each party has the right to interpose an objection to the reception of any item of evidence offered against him on the ground that it is irrelevant or that it falls within one or more of these exceptions or qualifications. There can be and is no question that the judge must either overrule or sustain every such objection, that is, he must rule that the jury may or may not hear the questioned testimony or see the proffered object. Where its admissibility does not depend upon the truth of a disputed proposition of fact, there is no problem of distribution of function between judge and jury. If he sustains the objection, the jury has no opportunity to hear or see the evidence; if he overrules the objection, the jury uses the admitted evidence as if no objection had been made. For example, in an action for breach of contract a defendant has denied only the making of the promise, and at

[8] THAYER, PRELIMINARY TREATISE ON EVIDENCE AT THE COMMON LAW 266 (1898).

the trial he offers evidence of an accord and satisfaction. On P's objection on ground of irrelevancy, the judge will rule it irrelevant. Next, assume that P offers W to testify to an exchange of words between P and D, words of offer and acceptance. An objection on the ground of hearsay will be overruled. But if W's testimony were that one X told him that P and D exchanged those words, an objection on grounds of hearsay would be sustained. In each of these situations the judge's ruling is in no way dependent upon the truth of any other proposition of fact.

*Relevancy Dependent on Preliminary Fact* The situation is or seems less simple when two items of evidence have to be offered, either one of which by itself has no probative value or insufficient probative value to be admissible, but both of which in conjunction have the requisite value. Assume that fact A alone or fact B alone has no recognized logical relation to fact C, but the existence of both does have such a logical relation. For example, C is the fact that defendant made a specified false statement to plaintiff; A is the fact that defendant made the false statement; B, that it was communicated to plaintiff. When plaintiff offers evidence of A by $W^1$, defendant objects that it is irrelevant, and when plaintiff offers evidence of B by $W^2$, defendant makes a like objection. It is impossible to introduce both at the same time. Defendant insists that evidence of the one is inadmissible until the existence of the other has been established, and he quotes from the opinion in *Gorton v. Hadsell*[9] the proposition approved by

[9] 9 Cush. (Mass.) 508 (1852).

Thayer and Wigmore and repeated literally or in substance in numberless opinions:

> But it is the province of the judge, who presides at the trial, to decide all questions on the admissibility of evidence. It is also his province to decide any preliminary questions of fact, however intricate, the solution of which may be necessary to enable him to determine the other question of admissibility.

He points out that in that case, plaintiff had to prove a writing of designated content signed by five persons who were proprietors of a meeting house. The writing of designated content was offered. It was signed by five identified persons, but the proposition that they were proprietors was in dispute, and the court held that it was for the judge to decide whether the signers were proprietors. He cites also *Gila Valley, Globe and Northern Ry. v. Hall* [10] in which the Supreme Court of the United States made a similar statement without qualification. Plaintiff responds by the citation of a later Massachusetts case and cases from other states reaching a contrary result in like situations.[11] He urges the judge to follow these precedents or, at least, to adopt the New Hampshire doctrine which puts the matter in his discretion.[12]

Why are the authorities in conflict on this easily analyzed problem? Because the judge must rule on every objection to the admissibility of evidence, does it follow that in order to rule on the admissibility of evidence of A, if it is first offered, he must determine whether or not B exists, and, if

[10] 232 U.S. 94, 34 S. Ct. 229 (1914).

[11] Coghlan v. White, 236 Mass. 165, 128 N.E. 33 (1900).

[12] Dunklee v. Prior, 80 N.H. 270, 116 Atl. 138 (1922); Jenness v. Jones, 68 N.H. 475, 44 Atl. 607 (1896).

evidence of B is first offered, he must determine whether or not A exists? If both could be and were offered as a unit, there could be no objection on the ground of irrelevancy. Limitations of time and space prevent the offering of both simultaneously. The rule that "without exception nothing which is not logically relevant is admissible" does not contemplate that each item of evidence must of itself be unconditionally relevant when offered. The rule is as applicable to trial by the judge or court alone as to trial by a jury. Suppose that in a trial by the judge it was objected that evidence of A was inadmissible until the existence of B was proved and evidence of B was inadmissible until the existence of A was proved, and that there was no escape from the dilemma. The amused or indignant reaction of the judge hardly needs mention. The objection has no more merit in a jury case, merely because the tribunal consists of judge and jury. It is conceded that if the judge finds B, the existence of A is for the jury, and if he finds A, the existence of B is for the jury. That tribunal is quite as competent to decide one issue as the other. Can it be that many courts are solemnly saying that the proponent of the evidence can determine upon which of the issues his opponent can have a trial by jury? If the trial were by the judge, when the objection was made to evidence of A, he would require merely that the proponent convince him that adequate admissible evidence of B would be later introduced. He might also rule that the evidence as to B should precede that as to A.

The same procedure should be used in a jury trial. The

evidence is of a kind that the jury is deemed capable of evaluating. Neither adversary is given the power to deprive the other of a trial by jury of a question of fact affecting the merits. The preliminary question for the judge when the relevancy of A depends upon the existence of B, and the existence of both A and B is in dispute, is whether the proponent will offer or has offered evidence which will justify a finding of both A and B. Thus when he offers evidence of A, the question for the judge is whether the proponent is adequately prepared to offer and will offer admissible evidence which will justify the jury in finding B. If the formula of *Gorton v. Hadsell* is insisted upon—if the judge has to decide any preliminary question of fact necessary to enable him to determine the question of admissibility—the facts in the question should be the intention and ability of the proponent to offer the requisite evidence of B and not whether B exists.

*Competency Dependent on Preliminary Fact* So much for the situation where the relevancy of one fact depends upon the existence of another and evidence of the existence of both facts is offered. What of the situations where the objection is to the reception of concededly relevant evidence on the ground that the witness is disqualified, or the objector or the witness has a pertinent privilege, or that unprivileged evidence offered by a qualified unprivileged witness offends the hearsay rule, or the so-called best evidence rule, or some similar exclusionary rule? In each of these, admissibility may depend upon the answer to a disputed question of fact. To what extent is the *Gorton v. Hadsell* doctrine applied by the courts, and how far does our theory of jury trial require its application?

Three observations should be made at the outset: (1) the doctrine is no longer uniformly applied; (2) in determining whether it should be applied, the courts seem to make no discriminations based on the reasons ordinarily put forward to support the pertinent exclusionary rule; and (3) the decisions, as typical samples will show, reveal no consistently applied principle.

The cases which have given most difficulty are those in which the preliminary question on the answer to which admissibility depends is identical with an ultimate question to be answered by the jury on the merits. Many of these have dealt with the incompetency or privilege arising from the marital relationship. In *State v. Lee*[13] the defendant was on trial for murder. It was common ground that the offense had been committed by one Mack Lee, and that a witness called by the defendant was the wife of that Mack Lee. She offered to testify that defendant, who was using the name Fenner, was not her husband. On objection to her competency, the judge held a preliminary hearing, found she was defendant's wife, and refused to allow her to testify. This ruling was affirmed. The coincidence of the two questions did not affect the orthodox distribution of functions between judge and jury.

In an early New York case[14] plaintiff was suing defendant for having enticed away plaintiff's wife. Plaintiff's evi-

[13] State v. Lee, 127 La. 1077, 54 So. 356 (1911).

[14] Scherpf v. Szadeczky, 4 E.D. Smith 110 (Common Pleas for City and County of N.Y. 1855).

dence tended to show a common-law marriage between plaintiff and the woman. Defendant called the woman and offered to have her testify that she was not plaintiff's wife. The most that can be said for the court's opinion is that it is interesting. It first stated that on such an objection the court must rule "without any hypothetical assumptions" and "upon the evidence appearing in the case at the time the testimony is offered." This approaches the ridiculous. It means that if the plaintiff had offered the woman at the opening of the case to prove that defendant had enticed her, she would have been competent. Later the court said that both plaintiff's and defendant's contention required the court to make assumptions and concluded:

> The defendant has no right to call upon the Court to receive an offer which places them in any such position, or exposes their ruling to any such absurdities in its result. It is rather to be said, that when the competency of the witness depends upon the very fact in issue, the witness is never competent. The competency is in doubt by the very state of the case, and there is no mode of removing the doubt but by the verdict. If the plaintiff has given evidence which is *prima facie* sufficient, the witness is incompetent upon the proof given. If the plaintiff has not given such proofs, he should be non-suited. In neither case is the examination of the witness by the defendant proper. The embarrassment or hardship, if any, results from the very nature of the case, and the party who offers the witness must bear the consequences of a difficulty that cannot be overcome.

Of course, it would be unseemly to require the court to avoid absurdities by the painful process of careful analysis instead of assuming that the decision of the judge that the witness may testify compels the jury to find that she is not plaintiff's wife. The opinion fails to recognize that the judge determines only whether the jury shall hear the witness, and that testimony which may convince the judge may or may not be credited by the jury. Furthermore, it declares that the judge may not hold a preliminary hearing upon the preliminary question. A similar result was reached in an early Canadian case.

The problem has frequently arisen in prosecutions for bigamy. *Miles v. United States*[15] is a leading case. Evidence was introduced that defendant had married Emily before the date on which, as he admitted, he married Caroline. When Caroline was called as a witness, defendant offered to prove his marriage to her as a basis for his objection to her competency. The trial judge permitted Caroline to give testimony tending to prove defendant's marriage to Emily. In holding this ruling erroneous, the Supreme Court said that the trial judge should have determined whether Emily was defendant's wife. The second wife is competent only where the first marriage is not disputed or has been established by other evidence. If the judge finds the first marriage subsisting, then the second wife is competent, she may testify to the second marriage but not to the first, "she cannot be permitted to prove a fact to the jury which must be established before she can testify at all." This is a curious qualification. The jury, which has nothing to do with the qualification of the witness, is prevented from hearing evidence relevant upon the merits

[15] 103 U.S. 304, 313–315 (1880).

merely because it is also relevant upon a question of competency already decided by the judge.

The same identity of the preliminary question and an ultimate question may occur where the ground of incompetency of the witness is other than marital relationship. And a similar problem may be presented when the admissibility of a hearsay declaration depends upon the qualification or identity of the declarant. In *Doe dem. Jenkins v. Davies*,[16] defendant's title depended upon the legitimacy of Elizabeth Stevens, deceased. Evidence of a statement by Elizabeth concerning her mother's marriage to Davies was admitted over objection. In holding the ruling correct, Lord Denman said that certain conditions must be fulfilled before evidence is admissible for the jury.

> The Judge alone has to decide whether the condition has been fulfilled. If the proof is by witnesses, he must decide on their credibility. If counter-evidence is offered, he must receive it before he decides; and he has no right to ask the opinion of the jury on the fact as a condition precedent.

To the objection that the issue was for the jury, and "if she was decided to be legitimate, her declarations to prove her legitimacy were superfluous," he answered "that neither the admissibility nor the effect of the evidence is altered by the accident that the fact which is for the Judge as a condition precedent is the same fact which is for the jury in the issue." But in a similar case some twenty-four years later Lord Penzance ruled the declaration admissible upon evidence which had been presented on the merits before

[16] 10 Q.B. 314 (1847).

the declarations were offered and for purely practical reasons refused to hear testimony from the objector on the preliminary question.[17]

In some situations a superficial analysis results in a mistake as to the tenor of the preliminary question. The problem raised when a proponent offers secondary evidence of a writing and the opponent objects and tenders what he claims to be the original writing is often misunderstood. In *Boyle v. Wiseman*[18] the court thought, or seemed to think, that it was for the judge to determine whether the opponent's document was in fact the original. The real issue was whether the proponent had accounted for the writing which he claimed to be the original. If he gave evidence of the existence of a paper bearing certain words and evidence which satisfied the judge that he could not produce the original of that paper for a good reason, the situation was the same as to the original as if he had presented one document and his opponent another. It would then be for the jury to determine which was the original. So here it was for the jury to determine whether there was such an original, and for the judge to determine whether the failure to produce that original, if any, was satisfactorily explained. So provide the Model Code of the American Law Institute and the Uniform Rules of Evidence. The few cases are in conflict.

The cases dealing with evidence of the conduct of one alleged conspirator offered against his alleged co-conspirator require but usually fail to receive careful analysis. The

[17] Hitchins v. Eardley, L.R. 2 P. & D. 248 (1871).
[18] 11 Exch. 360 (1855).

existence of a conspiracy between A and B may be shown by evidence of the individual and separate conduct of each which is a basis for a reasonable inference that the conduct was a result of an agreement, a conspiracy between them and not of mere coincidence. If such an agreement is found, then B is responsible for any conduct of A done in furtherance of the agreement or conspiracy, whether it be verbal or nonverbal, and, if verbal, whether it be hearsay or nonhearsay. But evidence of hearsay statements by A, like evidence of other conduct by A, not done in furtherance of the conspiracy is not admissible against B.

When B is on trial for an act done by A, the question whether it was done in furtherance of a conspiracy between A and B is for the jury. On that issue the question for the judge is whether the evidence would justify a reasonable jury in finding the conspiracy. When B is on trial for conspiring with A to do an act, the same is true. In both cases when evidence of a hearsay statement of A is offered against B, the preliminary question is whether the conspiracy has been established and whether the statement was made in furtherance thereof. It is not merely whether evidence has been received which would justify a finding. But many courts have mistaken the preliminary question, and held the hearsay admissible wherever the evidence, aside from the hearsay, would justify a finding of conspiracy. And many have added to the confusion by mistaking a statement concerning the conspiracy for a statement in furtherance of it.

Perhaps departure from orthodoxy ought to have been anticipated in situations where the question must ultimately be decided by the jury. This circumstance would call for reception, not exclusion, of the evidence. The desirability of avoiding a hearing before the judge of evidence, much of which might have to be repeated later before the jury, and the argument, that if the jury has to answer the question ultimately it should be held capable of answering it as a preliminary matter, might have been expected to appeal to so-called common sense. But the departure has gone further. In Massachusetts in criminal prosecutions, under what has been called "the humane practice in this Commonwealth," the preliminary question must first be decided by the judge. If he finds in favor of the objecting defendant, the evidence is rejected; if in favor of the proponent, the evidence is received, but the same question is put to the jury in the charge with instructions that unless they answer the preliminary question against the defendant, they must cast out the evidence. Thus if a witness for the Commonwealth is challenged as being too immature to understand the nature of the oath or equivalent sanction, or evidence of a dying declaration is objected to on the ground that declarant did not realize that death was speedily impending, or evidence of a confession on the ground that it was improperly induced, and the judge finds in favor of the proponent, he must in his charge instruct the jury that unless they answer the preliminary question against defendant's contention, they must cast out the evidence.

The result of the application of this doctrine in prosecutions for conspiracy is difficult to characterize with due deference to the judiciary. The jury is instructed that they cannot use the evidence of the separate conduct of A or his hearsay statements against B unless upon the other evidence in the case they have found that B conspired with A as charged in the indictment. If the trial judge is very careful, and knows of the decision in a well-considered case, he will explain that on the preliminary question the burden is on the Commonwealth to prove the conspiracy by a preponderance of the evidence but on the ultimate question it is to prove the conspiracy ultimately beyond a reasonable doubt. Of course, if he prescribes the latter measure of persuasion for the preliminary finding, it is not reversible error because in the defendant's favor. In the reported cases the trial judge has made no such distinction, so that if it be conceded that the jury could and did obey the instructions, they could have used the questioned evidence only to reassure themselves that their previously found verdict had additional support.

In some jurisdictions the language of the opinions may well be interpreted as asserting that the judge may, but need not, make the preliminary finding. But in most instances where the judge has given the jury the required instruction, it is impossible to tell whether or not he has made any preliminary finding, for he has merely overruled the objection to the evidence. If he has held the preliminary hearing outside the presence of the jury, he may have decided the question or he may have determined merely that a reasonable trier could find either way. In a few jurisdictions it is definitely held that the judge should submit the question to the jury wherever the evidence would justify a finding for the proponent. In New York this is now true with reference to a confession alleged to have been improperly induced.[19] There is as yet no tendency to extend either of these rules to civil cases, though a stray dictum or two may be found looking in that direction, and a few cases may be interpreted as approving the unconditional reception of the evidence wherever a trier might reasonably find the existence of the preliminary fact.

If this conglomeration of inconsistent holdings, running the gamut from strict enforcement of the orthodox view to its complete abandonment (Maguire and Epstein[20] found seven varieties), is to be tolerated, it must be because the division of function between judge and jury in the application of the rules governing the competence and privilege of witnesses and the rules excluding relevant evidence from unprivileged sources is of no appreciable importance. If so, the New Hampshire doctrine which puts the whole matter within the discretion of the trial judge is ideal. But the courts which reverse the trial judge for not applying the rule approved in the particular jurisdiction cannot make such a concession. As long as each of these exclusionary rules is judicially considered to have a rational basis, and as long as the division of function governing the determination of their applicability is judicially deemed of major importance, the determination as to each rule should depend upon the reason which supports it.

It is generally agreed that the judge is ordinarily under no duty to enforce an exclusionary rule except upon re-

[19] People v. Weiner, 248 N.Y. 118, 161 N.E. 441 (1928); Stein v. New York, 346 U.S. 156, 172 (1953).

[20] *Preliminary Questions of Fact, in Determining the Admissibility of Evidence,* 40 HARV. L. REV. 392 (1927).

quest or objection by a party or by the holder of a privilege. It is likewise recognized that it would be entirely impracticable to have the preliminary question tried in a separate hearing by the jury before the ruling on admissibility. To hold that wherever there is a bona fide dispute as to the existence of the preliminary fact the evidence is to be unconditionally admitted is to set up an entirely new rule. The choice, therefore, is between (1) a decision by the judge alone, the orthodox doctrine, and (2) a decision by the judge subject, however, to a later decision by the jury when the evidence is admitted, and (3) a decision by the jury during their deliberations upon the merits.

If the ground of incompetence of a witness is a social policy which has no relation to his trustworthiness, the third choice is rationally impossible. To permit or compel the person to testify is to destroy the foundation of the rule. For example, if, as the Second Circuit still holds, the policy of preserving marital harmony prevents one spouse from testifying when called by the prosecution in a criminal case in which the other spouse is the sole defendant, the damage is done as soon as the testimony is given. It cannot be repaired. The second choice is possible, for the damage will be greater if the testimony is used against the defendant, and the situation is no worse than if the judge's ruling had been final, though it may be fatuous to assume that jurors will or can disregard evidence which they have heard and deem trustworthy. The same is true where the existence of a privilege to have relevant evidence excluded depends upon the existence of a designated confidential relationship; for example, that of husband and wife, attorney and client, priest and penitent, or physician and patient. The privilege is that the confidential matter be not revealed, not that it be not used against the holder of the privilege or any other. In all these situations the effect of a conditional ruling against the objector would be the same if the trial were by the judge alone; to have him hear the evidence *de bene* would destroy the value of the rule.

If the ground of incompetence of the witness is his untrustworthiness, which at common law was thought to exist in many situations, the right of the objector is, on analysis, that he be not exposed to the danger that the trier of fact be misled by the testimony. This is his right also as to hearsay testimony offered through competent witnesses. It will be conceded that the danger, and the importance of eliminating it, are greater where the trier is a jury. Each of the exceptions to the hearsay rule is said or assumed to be based on the theory that the danger is so reduced as to be insubstantial by the circumstances affecting the declarant at the time of the hearsay conduct. If there is a dispute as to the disqualifying fact or as to the circumstances of the hearsay, the orthodox doctrine gives the objector full protection where the judge excludes the evidence. He gets a further theoretical protection if the jury is permitted to reexamine the question when the judge admits the evidence. Since the exclusion in these cases is to prevent the use of the evidence, not to guard against disclosure, he may get some slight protection by the third choice, which in effect gives the jury an instruction as to the value of the evidence.

Whether the exclusionary rule is based on a policy which creates a right to suppress the truth or on the right of a party to protection against the danger that the jury be misled, the adoption of the second choice (particularly under the practice in most jurisdictions which forbids the judge to comment on the weight of the evidence or the credibility of the witnesses) is likely to lead the trial judge to be less thorough in his consideration of the preliminary issue, since he can pass the responsibility on to the jury. It will be only where the evidence is pretty heavily in favor of exclusion that he will sustain the objection. And the result will be, first, in practice, and then, in legal theory, the adoption of the third choice. This is what has happened in criminal cases in a number of jurisdictions. The doctrine which began as a Massachusetts heresy has become orthodox in a large number of jurisdictions, perhaps the majority. The uncertainty of the judicial language has made some commentators and some trial judges interpret a number of decisions as approving the third choice, and a few decisions do so expressly. In short any departure from the orthodox view is likely to make the exclusionary rule degenerate into a rule concerning the value of the evidence, for to expect a jury actually to go through the process of separating the inadmissible evidence from the admissible and to eliminate its effect from their conscious minds and base their decision upon the admissible evidence only is to expect the impossible. Insofar as an instruction of this sort serves any purpose, it affects value, not admissibility.

If this process should eventuate in the abolition of the

remaining incompetencies of witnesses and the admissibility of all hearsay having appreciable probative value, it would accomplish at long last what should be accomplished speedily by legislation. Only a few incompetencies remain and the Uniform Rules of Evidence propose their extinction. The exceptions to the hearsay rule are increasing and the Uniform Rules would broaden their base. As to privileges, insofar as they are worth preserving, the orthodox rule should be retained. Insofar as they are unwise, they should be eliminated or modified by direct action.

The case of a confession induced by physical or mental coercion deserves special mention. The protection which the orthodox rule or the Massachusetts doctrine affords the accused is of major value to him. A fair consideration of the evidence upon the preliminary question is essential; in this consideration the truth or untruth of the confession is immaterial. Due process of law requires that a coerced confession be excluded from consideration by the jury. It also requires that the issue of coercion be tried by an unprejudiced trier, and, regardless of the pious fictions indulged by the courts, it is useless to contend that a juror who has heard the confession can be uninfluenced by his opinion as to the truth or falsity of it. Neither the due process clause of the Federal Constitution nor any other of its provisions requires any particular division of function between judge and jury. The result is that in New York and in a few other jurisdictions, the orthodox rule has been abandoned in the one situation where it is most needed. The rule excluding a coerced confession is more than a rule excluding hearsay. Whatever may be said about the orthodox reasoning that its exclusion is on the ground of its probable falsity, the fact is that the considerations which call for the exclusion of a coerced confession are those which call for the protection of every citizen, whether he be in fact guilty or not guilty. And the rule of exclusion ought not to be emasculated by admitting the evidence and giving to the jury an instruction which, as every judge and lawyer knows, cannot be obeyed.

The conclusion of this whole matter is that in the administration of trial by jury we deprive jurors of the effective assistance of the judge in the very situations where it is most needed. It is time that we ceased our inconsistent attitudes towards them—treating them at times as a group of low-grade morons and at other times as men endowed with a superhuman ability to control their emotions and intellects.

# HISTORY AND THEORY OF THE HEARSAY RULE

THE ORIGIN of the hearsay rule and the reasons given for its creation are revealed in the reported cases of the 1600s and in the discussions of the early text-writers. These I shall consider first. In seeking a principle upon which existing law as to hearsay is based, it is essential to analyze in some detail the process of proof under our system and to examine the pertinent decisions with a view to discovering the theory or theories which they seem or purport to apply. This task I shall undertake, but with little expectation of success.

I

*History* Thayer has said that the English law of evidence is the child of the jury; Wigmore and Holdsworth agree, but none of them supports the statement by detailed discussion. If it means that it was in the evolution of trial by jury in England that the testimony of witnesses in open court was first used as a means of furnishing jurors with the information to be used to reach a rational solution of the issue, and that rules governing the manner of giving the testimony and its content were incidentally required, it is true enough. But if it means, as frequently interpreted, that the rules which exclude relevant information from intelligent persons, and particularly the hearsay rule, owe their origin to a distrust of the jury's capacity to evaluate evidence, it has little, if any, support in history.

There can be no doubt that when trial by jury took a place beside the older forms of trial in England, there was no thought that the jury must base its verdict on first-hand information. The jurors were free to consult any source which they deemed reliable, and, indeed, were expected to supplement, before their appearance in court, what personal knowledge they had concerning the facts by inquiry of others, including the parties. While the early jurors may properly be characterized as "witnesses selected by a public officer," still they were not in any sense the kind of witnesses used in the earlier mode of trial known as trial by witnesses, in which the oaths of the witnesses as to what they had seen and heard, made with all due formality, were decisive. Nor were the jurors like preappointed witnesses such as deed witnesses or transaction witnesses, who were summoned with the jurors, went to the jury room with them, and were sworn to tell the truth and loyally inform the jury.

At the stage which corresponds to the modern trial, counsel for the parties made, or, as the records say, "showed in evidence," long recitals of fact—made them not as mere statements of claim, but as assertions which they asked the jurors to rely upon in corroboration of or in addition to what they already knew. From the beginning relevant writings were shown to the jury—deeds, wills, contracts, entries in registers and in books of parsons and stewards. And there was no attempt to separate the hearsay in them from the nonhearsay. Dying declarations and hearsay statements, as well as reputation, concerning family history in cases involving pedigree were constantly presented to the jury as information upon which to base the verdict.

When, during the 1400s, the parties acquired the privilege of offering evidence through witnesses, it may be probable, as Thayer believed, that these witnesses became confused with the earlier sorts of witnesses, and the courts expected them to speak only of what they had seen or heard. There was no tendency to confuse them with jurors who not only performed the functions of witnesses but also resolved the issue of fact. The oath of the jurors in effect required them to answer only to the best of their knowledge; that of the witnesses obligated them to tell the truth. But if the witnesses were ever forbidden to testify to hearsay, the restriction was short-lived. Wigmore is supported by an abundance of judicial rulings in his conclusion that "through the 1500's and down beyond the middle of the 1600's hearsay statements are constantly received, even against opposition." [1] Only occasionally are they rejected. In the 1500s the debate concerned not their admissibility but their evidential value. Even after the rule excluding hearsay was generally accepted (say in the last quarter of the 1600s), hearsay was received as corroborative evidence, and there was still hesitation about rejecting sworn hearsay.

During the latter part of the 1400s the use of witnesses was not uncommon, but as Fortescue informs us, their testimony was regarded as of minor importance. The jurors relied almost entirely upon what they knew or had learned

[1] 5 Wigmore, Evidence §1364, p. 15 (3d ed. 1940).

from other sources. The controversy in the latter part of the 1500s over the weight to be given to hearsay indicates that testimony at the trial was becoming of constantly increasing consequence. And by the time Coke wrote in the early 1600s, evidence presented in court furnished most of the materials for decision, but Bushell's Case [2] makes clear that as late as 1670 jurors had the right to disregard testimony in conflict with what they believed to be the facts from information they had acquired from other sources before being sworn. In fact it was not until near the middle of the eighteenth century that the present restrictions upon the sources of information usable by the jury were firmly established.

Thus by that time the jury had been transformed from a body chosen by the court to determine what the facts were from their own knowledge and from such sources as they deemed reliable without any control by the parties to a body which must depend solely on materials presented in court—most if not all of them by the parties. In other words, the sources of usable information were transferred from the control of the jury to the control of the parties.

*Early Reasons* What reasons were given for the rule excluding hearsay in the early years of its application? In 1684, L. C. J. Jeffries in the trial of Bradden and Speake for a misdemeanor rejected defendant's offer of evidence of what a declarant had said. "Why," he exclaimed, "if that woman were here herself, if she did say it and would not swear it, we could not hear her; how then can her saying

[2] Vaughan 135, 149 (1670).

be an evidence before us?"[3] Chief Baron Gilbert, whose treatise was written before 1726, likewise bases exclusion upon lack of oath:

> The attestation of the witness must be to what he knows, and not to that only which he hath heard, for mere hearsay is no evidence; for it is his knowledge that must direct the Court and Jury in the judgment of the fact, and not his mere credulity, which is very uncertain and various in several persons; for testimony being but an appeal to the knowledge of another, if indeed he doth not know, he can be no evidence; besides, though a person testify what he hath heard upon oath, yet the person who spake it was not upon oath; and if a man had been in court and said the same thing and had not sworn it, he had not been believed in a court of justice; . . .[4]

But both of these learned justices apparently overlooked the case noted in *Rolle's Abridgement* in 1668 in which sworn hearsay was rejected because "the other party could not cross-examine the party sworn, which is the common course."[5] And the learned Chief Baron, if he was writing after 1696, failed to consider the decision of the King's Bench in 1696, in which sworn hearsay was offered against a defendant:

> The Court thereupon sent the *puisne judge* to confer with the Justices of the Common Pleas; who, returning, THE CHIEF JUSTICE declared, that it was the opinion of both Courts that these depositions should not be given in evidence, the defendant not being present when they were taken before the mayor, and so had lost the benefit of a cross-examination.[6]

[3] 9 HOWELL'S STATE TRIALS p. 1189, col. 1.
[4] GILBERT, THE LAW OF EVIDENCE 152 (2d ed. 1760).
[5] 2 Roll. Abr. 679, pl. 9 (1668).
[6] 6 Rex v. Paine, 5 Mod. 163, 165 (K.B. 1696).

But Serjeant Hawkins in 1716 in his *Pleas of the Crown* advances both reasons: "It seems agreed, that what a Stranger has been heard to say is in Strictness no manner of Evidence either for or against a Prisoner, not only because it is not upon Oath but also because the other Side hath no opportunity of a cross-examination." [7] In Bacon's *Abridgement* in 1736 the lack of oath is mentioned first and the lack of opportunity for cross-examination is given as an additional reason for rejecting "what another has been heard to say."

Blackstone, treating the subject of evidence very briefly, apparently accepts Gilbert's view for he refers to Gilbert's work as an excellent treatise of evidence which cannot be summarized without marring it. MacNally in 1802 in his *Rules of Evidence on Pleas of the Crown* [8] adopts the statement of Hawkins. Peake in 1822, referring to his first edition of 1801, asserts that when he first turned his attention to evidence there was nothing before the profession but the "unfinished publication of Lord C. B. Gilbert and the little more than a copy of it by Mr. Justice Buller." [9] He gives as the reasons for rejecting hearsay only the lack of oath and lack of opportunity for cross-examination. Starkie in both the 1824 and 1833 editions of his treatise does likewise. And the same is true of Roscoe's work on *Criminal Evidence* published in 1835.

In this country, Chief Justice Marshall in 1813 in refusing to extend the pedigree exception to declarations as to

[7] Book II, c. 46, sec. 14.
[8] Book II, c. II, p. 360.
[9] Peake, A Compendium of the Law of Evidence, Preface to fifth London ed. (1822).

free or slave status declared: "Its intrinsic weakness, its incompetency to satisfy the mind of the existence of the fact and the frauds which might be practised under its cover, combine to support the rule that hearsay evidence is totally inadmissible." [10] For these reasons he pointed out that the decisions treating the hearsay rule as merely one requiring the best available evidence were inapplicable.

It is, therefore, abundantly clear that the reasons for rejecting hearsay given by judges and commentators at the time the rule was becoming established have to do with the credulity not of jurors but of witnesses, the absence of the sanction of an oath, and lack of opportunity to cross-examine. And this view was generally accepted during the following century in England. Chief Justice Marshall added the theory that hearsay is intrinsically of no appreciable probative value and is subject to fraudulent invention. Each of these reasons is as applicable to one sort of tribunal as to another. Not one of them even suggests a peculiar incapacity of jurors to evaluate such evidence, and so long as jurors could properly rely upon what they had learned by inquiry or otherwise outside the presence of the court, any such suggestion would have bordered on absurdity.

There was no requirement of actual cross-examination by the adversary. He could waive cross-examination, and it seems that the same was true as to the oath. Consequently, under the rule accurately stated, the adversary's right was to have excluded from consideration testimony not given under the sanction of an oath and subject to

[10] Mima Queen v. Hepburn, 11 U.S. (7 Cranch) 290, 296 (1813).

cross-examination. This must mean that when such evidence was tendered the adversary had to make known his demand that it be not received, and this necessarily raised the question as to who should decide upon the validity of his demand, the judge or the jury. Consequently rules governing the respective functions of judge and jury had to be evolved. These rules would obviously have been unnecessary in a trial before a judge alone. But they would have been equally unnecessary had the adversary not gained such a large measure of control over the sources of available evidence and the right to cross-examine, a right unknown to systems of trial other than the common-law system.

There is nothing in the history of the English equity processes for securing evidence that throws any light on the problem. While the common-law rule was being developed, the equity practice was making more difficult the task of evaluating testimony in equity. After the pleadings were closed, counsel for the party desiring to take testimony of a witness and counsel for the adversary drafted questions to be answered by the witness before a clerk or commissioners. Neither disclosed to the other the questions so drafted. The answers were taken in private without the presence of the parties, and the clerk or commissioners and assistants were sworn to secrecy. The questions and answers were engrossed on parchment and duly returned and filed. Thereafter an order for their publication was made, and the answers were for the first time available to counsel. The questions framed by the adversary's counsel in ignorance of everything except the issues made under the pleadings could scarcely be called cross-examination. The oath of the witness, as at common law, required him to tell the truth, the whole truth, and nothing but the truth. And unless specific questions submitted asked the source of the information upon which he based his answer, there was nothing to show that his information was first hand. In none of the contemporary discussions is there any suggestion of superior capacity of the chancellor or his substitutes to evaluate such evidence, while there can be no doubt that in the Ecclesiastical Courts and courts administering the Roman law there was no rule excluding hearsay.

*Early Distrust of Jury* It must be recognized, however, that from a comparatively early date in the development of jury trial, both counsel and judges manifested increasing distrust of jurors in dealing with materials for decision in two respects. First, their ability to deal with questions of law. In civil cases the jury's function was early limited to matters of fact. Though this had its origin in the efforts of the jurors themselves to escape liability for punishment for a false verdict, the capacity of a layman to learn and understand rules of law could not long remain unquestioned. Second, their ability to distinguish the legally important from the legally unimportant and to remember and apply the former. As to this we find counsel endeavoring to get into the record by way of the pleadings much that could properly be deemed merely evidential, and, later, the English judges attempting to compel the jurors to render special verdicts or answer specific interrogatories as to particular facts. This latter, as we know, led to the great controversy which resulted in Fox's Libel Act, a statute much misunderstood both in England and in this country. Finally, the sole common-law method of reviewing the jury's decision on the facts was by attaint. The loser, on demand and payment of the prescribed fee, could have the same question of fact submitted to a jury of larger number and higher rank, whose answer would be final. In the 1600s, at the period when the hearsay rule was being evolved, the judges found that the attaint jury instead of considering the question which the original jury had answered, in fact substituted for it the question whether the original jurors had given their answer honestly and in good faith, and usually merely affirmed the original verdict. This caused the judges to declare that the attaint had become a mere sound and to grant new trials where verdicts seemed to them demonstrably wrong on the facts. This practice began shortly after the middle of the 1600s and became more frequent after Bushell's case had made it clear that a judge could not punish jurors for refusing to obey his directions as to the facts. Near the end of the 1600s an occasional case of a directed verdict is found, and by the middle of the eighteenth century the power of the court to direct a verdict in civil cases was pretty well established.

*Wright v. Tatham* It is scarcely to be wondered at, therefore, that in the 1800s when the judges were attempting to rationalize the rules of evidence and were confronted with the task of justifying the rejection in court of matter which men of common sense would consider of great value in determining the truth or untruth of a proposition of fact, they should turn to the supposed frailty of jurors. The leading case, *Wright v. Tatham,* was finally decided in 1838.[11] There the court was urged to hold admissible evidence of conduct of third persons as tending to prove their opinions that the testator was sane. After analyzing the evidence as amounting to a hearsay statement of the observed conduct of the testator, the judges felt it necessary in justifying its exclusion to deal with hypothetical situations pressed upon them by counsel in which the hearsay was of particularly persuasive force, and to distinguish contrary rulings in the Ecclesiastical Courts on the identical problem.

In the Exchequer Chamber, Baron Parke in dealing with the Ecclesiastical precedents pointed out that they did not conform to common-law rules, and added: "Some greater laxity may be permitted in a Court which adjudicates both on the law and on the fact, and may be more safely trusted with consideration of such evidence than a jury." Baron Bosanquet likewise:

> Where the Judges are authorized to deal both with the facts and the law, a much larger discretion with respect to the reception of evidence may not unreasonably be allowed than in Courts of Common Law, where the evidence, if received by the Judge, must necessarily be submitted entire to the jury. By the rules of evidence established in the Courts of Law, circumstances of great moral weight are often excluded, from which much assistance might in particular cases be afforded in coming to a just conclusion, but which are nevertheless withheld from the consideration of the jury upon general principles, lest they should produce an

[11] Wright v. Doe d. Tatham, 5 Cl. & Fin. 670 (House of Lords 1838); 7 A. & E. 313 (Exch. Chamb. 1837).

undue influence upon the minds of persons unaccustomed to consider the limitations and restrictions which legal views upon the subject would impose.

On writ of error to the House of Lords in which the opinions of all the judges and barons were given, most of them agreed that the presence of a jury in courts of common law made the ecclesiastical cases inapplicable. Chief Justice Tindall went so far as to say:

> From the peculiarity of the tribunal of the Courts of the Common Law have arisen nine parts out of ten of the peculiarities of our law of evidence. Here the principle of admissibility of evidence must be founded on the peculiarity of the tribunal to which it is tendered.

And Mr. Justice Coleridge in answering a contention of counsel uttered one of the most incomprehensible propositions to be found in the books. He declared it to be "based on the fallacy, that, whatever is morally convincing, and whatever reasonable beings would form their judgments and act upon, may be submitted to a jury."

Thereafter the likelihood that jurors may be misled by hearsay which does not fall within a recognized exception has been frequently put forward as a reason for refusing to create new exceptions. Consequently it may fairly be said that while distrust of the jury had nothing to do with the origin of the hearsay rule, it has exerted a strong influence in preventing or delaying its liberalization.

II

So much for the origin of the rule. What of the theory of its application and exceptions?

*Precedent* The hearsay involved in the early cases fell within the description of Serjeant Hawkins's "what a Stranger has been heard to say." Before the early 1800s there was practically no attempt to support the rulings which received such evidence by reasons specifically applicable to the utterance in question. Mr. Justice Buller in *Regina v. Eriswell,*[12] decided in 1790, put it frankly:

> The true line for the courts to adhere to is, that, wherever evidence not on oath has been repeatedly received, and sanctioned by judicial determination, it shall be allowed; but beyond that, the rule, that no evidence shall be admitted, but what is upon oath, shall be observed.

Lord Kenyon agreed as to the force of precedent, but added:

> All questions upon the rules of evidence are of vast importance to all orders and degrees of men; our lives, our liberty, and our property are all concerned in the support of these rules, which have been matured by the wisdom of ages, and are now revered from their antiquity and the good sense in which they are founded; they are not rules depending on technical refinements but upon good sense; and the preservation of them is the first duty of judges.

As to whether the particular evidence in the case at bar was properly admitted, these learned judges disagreed. Neither talked of the function of cross-examination or considered the inherent value of the offered hearsay, or any circumstances that would make it more or less easy to appraise than ordinary hearsay, or any virtues or faults in it which made oath or cross-examination or both necessary or unnecessary. Precedent alone was decisive.

[12] Regina v. Eriswell, 3 T.R. 707, 719, 721 (1790).

But if we are to have a rational system, we cannot accept ancient procedural precedents as having been divinely inspired or be deterred from questioning them by assurances that they had as early as 1790 been matured by the wisdom of the ages and are to be revered not only because of their antiquity but also because of their foundation in good sense (and particularly when the assurance comes from Lord Kenyon, whom Thayer once described as "famously ignorant"). Are we to continue to admit hearsay that falls within these precedents and reject all other hearsay? Should we not examine the decisions of modern courts to discover the reasons upon which they base the exclusion of hearsay and to determine to what extent they should be applied? This requires consideration of the means by which materials for decision are made available to the trier of fact and an elementary analysis of the intellectual operations required in using those materials in resolving an issue. As to each proposition of fact which is disputable and disputed the trier must rely upon what occurs in his presence in the course of the trial. This will never be the matter in dispute, no matter how close may be the connection between the two. From what he perceives he must draw inferences which lead to conclusions concerning events or conditions in the past.

*Elementary Analysis* Suppose that the proponent desires to convince the trier that event X happened and calls a witness whom he expects to testify that such was the case. What the trier sees is the witness on the stand and counsel facing the witness; he hears counsel utter a series of sounds, followed by another sound or series of sounds uttered by the witness. Trier must first determine what words were formed by those sounds. Assume that those uttered by Witness seemed to Trier to form the sentence, "I perceived X." If so, the next question for Trier is, did Witness actually utter those words? If so, did he in uttering them intend to convey to Trier the information that those words would convey if Trier had used them himself? If not, what did Witness intend to communicate to Trier? Until Trier answers this question, the testimony of Witness is useless. Of course, Trier does not usually take these two steps consciously; he ordinarily assumes that what he seems to hear is what he actually hears and that Witness is using language in what Trier considers to be its usually accepted meaning. But in many instances one or the other of these assumptions may be false. The proponent may have framed his question with meticulous accuracy and the witness may have done likewise with his response for reasons not disclosed, or if disclosed not fully comprehended by the trier. Take two examples from the trial of Sacco and Vanzetti for the murder of Berardelli in a holdup in September, 1920.

Captain Van Amburgh testifying on direct examination as to the cause of certain pitting in the barrel of Sacco's pistol: "I really believe that it is by allowing powder fowling to stand in the barrel, and the matter of rust allowed to stand and eat its way, and finally pits occur."

On cross-examination, he used "believe" and "inclined to believe," but finally said, "I believe it has been caused by rust."

*Q*. "When you say, 'I believe,' have you anything back of that that you don't quite feel sure of?"

*A.* "Yes, I have a slight reservation. I have known pitting to be in metal when it came from the mill, and it was due to a flaw or some little imperfection in the metal, and, therefore, I would not say every time I see a pit in such a piece of metal it was caused by rust. . . . That, I believe, explains my reservation, mental reservation, on the matter of rust." [13]

On direct examination upon another point he had been asked: "Have you formed an opinion, Captain, as to whether or not No. 3 bullet was fired from that particular Colt automatic?"

*A.* "I have an opinion."

*Q.* "And what is your opinion?"

*A.* "I am inclined to believe that it was fired, No. 3 bullet was fired, from this Colt automatic pistol." [14]

There was no cross-examination upon "inclined to believe," but obviously it connotes greater uncertainty than "I really believe" or "I believe."

Captain Proctor was asked: "Have you an opinion as to whether bullet 3 was fired from the Colt automatic [Sacco's pistol] which is in evidence?"

*A.* "I have."

*Q.* "And what is your opinion?"

*A.* "My opinion is that it is consistent with being fired by that pistol." [15]

The trial judge in his charge and counsel for the defense so far as appears from their arguments to the jury under-

[13] 1 THE SACCO-VANZETTI CASE, TRANSCRIPT OF RECORD OF TRIAL OF NICOLA SACCO AND BARTOLOMEO VANZETTI IN THE COURTS OF MASSACHUSETTS AND SUBSEQUENT PROCEEDINGS 924 (1928).

[14] 1 *Id.* 920–21.

[15] 1 *Id.* 896.

stood that each of these witnesses had given the opinion that the bullet was actually fired from Sacco's pistol. What Van Amburgh had said made it clear that he had substantial doubts, but did the trier get the distinction between "believe" and "inclined to believe"? What Proctor actually meant and what the prosecution knew he meant but did not reveal to court or jury is shown by his later affidavit.

"At no time was I able to find any evidence whatever which tended to convince me that the particular model [mortal?] bullet found in Berardelli's body, which came from a Colt automatic pistol, . . . came from Sacco's pistol and I so informed the District Attorney and his assistant before the trial. . . . Had I been asked the direct question: whether I had found any affirmative evidence whatever that this so-called mortal bullet had passed through this particular Sacco's pistol, I should have answered then, as I do now without hesitation, in the negative." [16]

Here were skilled witnesses using language in a strictly accurate sense but in such a way that the trier would have to discriminate sharply between what he seemed to hear and precisely what he did hear and to consider carefully exactly what the witness intended to communicate to him. Where the witness is illiterate or unacquainted with idiomatic English or employs some usage peculiar to the locality of his residence but unknown to the trier, the dangers of misunderstanding and misinterpretation are obvious.

If Trier concludes that Witness intended to tell Trier that Witness had seen X, then Trier must determine whether Witness then and there believed that he had seen

[16] 4 *Id.* 3642–43.

X. If not, the testimony is useless as evidence of the occurrence of X. Is Trier to assume the sincerity of Witness where the testimony has no element of inherent improbability? If sincerity is assumed or found, the next question involves what is usually termed memory. Witness now has a mental picture of having perceived X. What causes him to have it? Did he at the time in question have the same mental picture or is he reconstructing the picture to conform to something that occurred later, or is he attributing to himself the experience of another?

In an attempted holdup robbery of a payroll truck of the White Shoe Co. on December 24, 1919, at 12:15 P.M., three bandits after vainly shooting at the truck escaped in an automobile.[17] In the afternoon of the same day, one Harding, an eyewitness, described to a Pinkerton detective each of the three, including the hats worn by them. As to the bandit with a shotgun, he said: "The man with the shot-gun was slim, 5′10″, wore a long black overcoat and a black derby hat. I did not get much of a look at his face." On December 31 he told another Pinkerton operative, "The man wearing the black coat was without a hat and his coat was very long." On January 3 he was unable to say to a third operative whether two men whom he had seen and described as of the same build as the bandits were in fact the gunmen because he had not seen the faces at the holdup. "These two men," he stated, "were both

[17] The text setting out excerpts from the descriptions given by Harding is based upon the Pinkerton Reports, the record of the preliminary hearing and the record of the trial of Vanzetti as printed in the *Supplemental Volume of The Sacco-Vanzetti Case* (see note 13 *supra*) 22–29; 366, 386, 388; 89–104.

dark complexioned, the taller of the two having a small short cropped moustache."

Vanzetti was arrested and charged as one of the bandits. In Harding's testimony at the preliminary hearing on May 18, *after* he had seen Vanzetti at the police station, he described the man with the shotgun as of "medium height, dark complected, a long black overcoat, and no hat. Hair cut close in back . . . . moustache that had been cropped off, not short and croppy, but a moustache that had been trimmed up. Not long and flowing, but shorter. Did you ever see moustaches that are small but not Charlie Chaplins but an overgrown Charlie Chaplin trimmed on the ends? . . . He was swarthy, dark complected. . . . He had high cheek bones . . . red cheeks."

At the trial more than a month later, he added "high forehead," "hair was short," "rather hard broad face and the head more of a round head bullet shaped," "a heavy dark moustache that had been trimmed, the ends had been cut off anyway, it was not a flowing moustache." And he asserted that he had got a "fairly good," "a very good look" at the bandit.

In these varying descriptions, which at first tend to agree in some details with descriptions given by some other eyewitnesses, and which, like those others as modified after Vanzetti's arrest, picture Vanzetti's appearance with increasing accuracy, how much is Harding reproducing details of his original mental picture and how much reconstructing that picture to conform to what the others believed they saw and to the impressions made by the more deliberate observation of Vanzetti?

In the Vanzetti case Harding did actually have the experience concerning which he testified. But what of this case? After the close of the Russo-Japanese War, a representative of one of the countries involved was in New England. There is no question that he visited the Harvard Law School when school was not in session, and that only one member of the Faculty had an interview with him in the Austin Hall stacks. There is no question that the one remarkable thing in the interview was his inquiry as to what was done when there was a student strike. Now each of two most distinguished scholars then on the faculty was later firmly of the opinion that he was the man with whom the representative had talked. No doubt, had either been called as a witness, he would have so sworn. Certainly one was attributing to himself an experience which the other had related to him and which he unconsciously appropriated as his own.[18]

Consequently, assuming the accuracy of the communication from Witness to Trier and the complete sincerity of Witness, Trier must deal with the asserted retention of the mental impression which the purported experience originally created.

If Trier comes to a conclusion as to the substantial accuracy of Witness in this respect, he still has to determine whether or to what extent that mental impression corresponded with what was actually open to the observation or perception of Witness. And here the chances of error are few or many depending upon the subject matter and

[18] *Ex relatione* of one of these distinguished scholars whose name I do not feel at liberty to disclose.

upon the perceptual capacities of Witness and his opportunity and stimuli to use them. The typical instance of mistakes in observation is that of mistaken identity, in which the mistake is established after the victim has paid all or part of the penalty caused by it. Other cases may be found where skill in observation is essential, as where a reputable physician, unskilled in reading X ray plates or films, identifies a dark patch on the film as a spot on the lung which in fact is the shadow of the aorta, or fails to identify a fine line as a fracture of the skull. Experiments conducted in the presence of a group of educated persons warned in advance to observe carefully have demonstrated startling inaccuracies in both vision and hearing.

For the data upon which he must base his decision then, Trier must determine and rely upon the language used by Witness, his sincerity or lack of it, his memory, and his perception. If Trier is a judge, he will have these things in mind; if a juror, he is likely not to be aware that any of them is subject to serious question unless this is brought to his attention. The sanction, moral and legal, of the obligation to tell the truth, and the realization that he may be cross-examined, will stimulate Witness to search his memory and to tell what he believes to be the truth insofar as it is called for by the questions put to him. They will affect the element of sincerity and nothing else. The mere opportunity for the adversary to cross-examine Witness will add nothing to the degree of dependability which may be placed upon his language as a means of communication, upon the quality of his memory, or upon his perception. Actual cross-examination skillfully conducted will disclose facts that will enable Trier to determine to what extent reliance may reasonably be put upon each of these elements.

It is too obvious for argument that if Witness testifies not, "I saw X," but, "Declarant told me that he saw X," and the issue is whether X happened, all that oath and cross-examination can accomplish will relate to the auditory experience of Witness, and that if Trier concludes that Witness did hear Declarant say that he saw X, there has been no opportunity to test the four elements upon which the evidential value of Declarant's statement depends except to the extent that the testimony of Witness may reveal. If it is to be received as tending to prove that X happened, the protection which the oath and opportunity for cross-examination afford the Adversary is gone; the risk that Trier may be misled is present in full force. The Declarant's language, sincerity, memory, and observation are all involved. And this was true in most, if not all, the early precedents. In *Wright v. Tatham*, however, the use of language was not involved, for the statements were not offered for the truth of anything stated therein and guaranties of the sincerity of the Declarant were in the discussion held immaterial unless buttressed by an oath.

*Limitations upon Adversary Theory* If the adversary is to be given full protection, all statements of a person not present and subject to cross-examination which are offered in evidence for a purpose which requires the Trier to rely upon that person's language, sincerity, memory, or perception must on his objection be held inadmissible. But he has never been given this full measure of protection. We may agree with the late Mr. Justice Jackson[19] that "a common law trial is and always should be an adversary proceeding," with his implication that it cannot be properly conducted except by members of a learned profession, and with his settled opinion that the rules should not enable counsel for either party to perform his functions "either without wits or on wits borrowed from the adversary." We must concede that the trial is a proceeding not for the discovery of truth as such, but for the establishment of a basis of fact for the adjustment of a dispute between litigants. Still it must never be forgotten that its prime objective is to have that basis as close an approximation to the truth as is practicable. The emphasis upon the protection of the adversary and the fact that the result is binding only upon the parties and their privies have tended to make this objective seem of secondary importance. Indeed it seems to be almost completely ignored in many of our trial courts, particularly where the judge by mandatory rule or self-imposed restriction may not reveal to the jury his opinion as to the facts. It cannot be too emphatically asserted that such a beclouding of the objective is an abandonment of the fundamental principle of the adversary system, namely, that each adversary because of his interest will be keen to discover and present materials showing the strength of his position and the weakness of his opponent's, so that the truth will emerge to the perception of the impartial tribunal. This definitely

[19] In his concurring opinion in Hickman v. Taylor, 329 U.S. 495, 67 S. Ct. 385 (1947).

is not to say that either adversary has a privilege to conceal or to prevent the disclosure of matter which would tend to make the truth apparent. And it is the function of the judge to regulate the conduct of the trial accordingly. The adversary may waive his right that the witness be sworn and also his right to cross-examine, but the judge may insist that the witness speak only under the prescribed sanctions. If the trial is by the judge, he may cross-examine fully, if by jury in England he may cross-examine just as vigorously, and in this country he may put questions that will bring out omitted material matter or matter clarifying what has been previously testified, so long as he does not indicate prejudice or his opinion as to the facts or the credibility of the witness. The hearsay rule, when applicable, gives each party the right not to bear the risk that the trier will be misled by the objectionable hearsay. He may have it excluded, but he has no right that it shall be admitted when offered by his opponent. The judge may of his own motion properly protect the jury from misleading testimony. The control of the adversary over the reception of evidence and other aspects of the trial is still limited.

*Confusion in the Precedents* In this setting, should all hearsay be excluded? As Chief Justice White was fond of saying, "To ask the question is to answer it."

Upon what principle then is admissibility or exclusion determined? Do the existing decisions provide any test for determining the effect upon admissibility of oath and opportunity to cross-examine or the lack of either or both? First, consider six situations where the person whose extrajudicial statement is offered is present before the trier of fact.

1. What is the effect of loss of opportunity for adequate cross-examination by the party against whom a witness has testified under oath in the presence of the trier confronting that party and expecting to be cross-examined by him? Is that party entitled to have the direct testimony stricken regardless of the cause of the loss? If the witness on cross-examination refuses to answer pertinent questions upon any matter in defiance of the judge's ruling, it seems obvious that he is trying to suppress at least a part of the truth and to make a misleading communication to the trier, and what he has therefore testified upon that matter should not be usable by the trier. The same is true where the judge sustains a claim of privilege by the witness. And it goes without saying that where the proponent by design or fault causes the loss, he cannot be allowed to have the benefit of the un-cross-examined testimony. But where the loss occurs without fault of the witness and without the exercise of any claim of privilege by him, and without any wrong or neglect of the proponent, is the risk that the trier may be misled so substantial that a statement made with all these safeguards should go for nought? The few American cases in point say so.[20] They do not discuss the reliability of the evidence or compare the risk which the objector incurs with that incurred in the recognized exceptions to the hearsay rule. Lack of opportunity to cross-examine is decisive.

2. Where a witness, who is present and subject to cross-examination and is ready and willing to testify upon a given

[20] See e.g., People v. Cole, 43 N.Y. 508 (1871).

matter from present memory, has previously made a statement concerning the same matter, is evidence of that statement offered to prove the truth of the matter stated to be excluded as hearsay?

Greenleaf and his subsequent editors through the first fifteen editions said, [21] ". . . hearsay denotes that kind of evidence which does not derive its value solely from the credit to be given to the witness himself, but rests also, in part, on the veracity and competency of some other person." Underhill adds this to his paraphrase of Greenleaf's sentence: "Its value, if any, is measured by the credit to be given to some third person not sworn as a witness to that fact, and consequently not subject to cross-examination." If the former statement is consistent with the present or proposed testimony, it may well be urged that the testimony under oath in the presence of the trier is to be preferred, and that the former statement is not only unnecessary but amounts or would amount to mere repetition. But as to the hearsay aspect, the safeguards which oath and cross-examination are designed to provide and all the factors which afford the trier, whether judge or jury, the means of evaluating the evidence seem to be present in full force. Yet Mr. Justice Stone of the Minnesota Supreme Court would not agree. He declared:

> The chief merit of cross examination is not that at some future time it gives the party opponent the right to dissect adverse testimony. Its principal virtue is in its immediate application of the testing process. Its strokes fall while the iron is hot. False testimony is apt to harden and become unyielding to the blows of

[21] 1 Greenleaf on Evidence §99 (15th ed. 1892), quoted with approval in State v. Crean, 43 Mont. 47, 114 Pac. 603 (1911).

truth in proportion as the witness has opportunity for reconsideration and influence by the suggestion of others, whose interest may be, and often is, to maintain falsehood rather than truth.[22]

This argument carries its own refutation, for it would apply most forcibly to the later testimony in court, which is never given until there has been ample time for reconsideration and influence by the suggestion of others. And what qualities of falsehood cause it to harden which are absent from truth? Of course, Mr. Justice Stone was attempting to support the accepted doctrine which rejects this evidence on the ground of hearsay. In the case before him, the former statement was inconsistent with the testimony, but the learned Justice put both consistent and inconsistent statements in the same category.

And for purposes of classification, he was right. Consider, first, the situation where the witness concedes that he made the prior statement, but now insists that he was then in error. As Judge Learned Hand said, in one of his more liberal attitudes toward judicial power to change outworn rules of evidence:

If, from all that the jury sees of the witness, they conclude that what he says now is not the truth, but what he said before, they are none the less deciding from what they see and hear of that person and in court. There is no mythical necessity that the case must be decided only in accordance with the truth of words uttered under oath in court.[23]

If the witness denies having made the prior statement, the trier has all the materials for decision upon that issue, in the same manner and to the same effect as if the utter-

[22] State v. Saporen, 205 Minn. 358, 362, 285 N.W. 898, 901 (1939).
[23] Di Carlo v. United States, 6 F.2d 364, 368 (2d Cir. 1925).

ance had no hearsay quality. If the denial is found true, there will be no further consideration of the statement. If the trier is persuaded by otherwise admissible evidence that the witness made the prior statement, the problem of the credit to be given to it as against his present testimony is exactly the same as if he had conceded making it, except that the trier has already decided that the witness has falsified or been mistaken as to one relevant matter.

Consequently none of the reasons which have been given to justify the creation or continued existence of the hearsay rule have any appreciable application to evidence of prior statements by a person who is present and subject to cross-examination as to the statement and the matter stated. The evidence derives its value solely from the credit to be given to the witness or witnesses. Its value is not measured by the credit to be given to any person not sworn as a witness and subject to cross-examination. It falls beyond the boundaries of hearsay as described by Greenleaf and Underhill. Nevertheless it is almost universally held to be inadmissible hearsay. Judge Hand's statement is made of no effect by the decision in *Bridges v. Wixon.*[24] And it makes no difference whether the prior statement is written or oral.

3. A witness who is present and subject to cross-examination and has testified concerning an event which he has perceived may testify also to a statement made by him which describes or explains that event if when he spoke he was laboring under the stress of a nervous excitement caused by his perception of the event. This is true in the great majority of jurisdictions. Some courts, accepting Thayer's

[24] 326 U.S. 135, 65 S. Ct. 1443 (1945).

theory, hold such a statement admissible if made while he was perceiving the event, whether or not it was exciting and whether or not he was nervously affected by his perception. These circumstances, which are deemed to make the statement spontaneous, not reflective, may indicate a lack of opportunity to fabricate, but it is scarcely necessary to point out that such a statement is never made under oath or subject to cross-examination. It is nothing more than a prior consistent statement by the witness, who at the time it is offered in evidence is subject to full cross-examination under oath. No reliance is placed on the opportunity to cross-examine.

4. Now assume that the former statement was a part of the testimony given by W as a witness for A at the trial of an action by A against B upon issue X, and that at a second trial of the same action, W is present and subject to cross-examination. If A offers the former testimony without calling W to the stand, the evidence will be rejected. This might be justified as an application of the best evidence principle, although there is a good argument that the earlier testimony is more likely to be accurate as having been given when W's memory of the subject matter was fresher, and, if the testimony is admitted, B may call W for cross-examination. If A calls W and W's present testimony is consistent with his former testimony, this argument as to fresher memory loses force, but if inconsistent, the argument has double strength. In any event, the reasons for excluding hearsay have no relevance. If B is objecting, he cannot show the absence of a single safeguard designed for his protection, for the statement was under oath and

is subject to a second opportunity for cross-examination under oath. Even under Mr. Justice Stone's reasoning, the evidence is unobjectionable insofar as its trustworthiness is concerned.

The earliest cases rejecting sworn hearsay assume that it would have been admissible had the adversary been afforded the opportunity to cross-examine. And in our assumed case, it is universally agreed that the evidence of the former testimony is receivable, if the witness is unavailable, though there is conflict as to what constitutes the requisite unavailability. But if the second trial is an action between C and B in which the same issue X is crucial, and C offers against B the former testimony of W, the orthodox rule requires its rejection. No argument has ever been made to the effect that the evidence is or can be affected in any quality involving any hearsay danger by the mere fact that the proponent is a new party, C, rather than the original offeror, A. Can an argument based on adversary theory be made? Consider this. If B were offering this evidence against C, C could effectively object that he had never had opportunity to cross-examine W. Suppose that after the issue is fully tried out in the action by A against B, all of the witnesses become unavailable by death before the action by C is tried. Is the former testimony of witnesses favorable to B to be excluded at this trial while that of the other witnesses is to be received? Would this be fair? Should not C have to carry the same risk as B of supervening loss of witnesses? Is not equality in the burden of risk an essential of our adversary system? Perhaps it is unnecessary to say that the judicial opinions do not contain any suggestion of such a contention. They drag in a totally different factor, namely, the doctrine of privity as applied to the effect of a judgment in the first action as res adjudicata in the second, a doctrine which has no logical or practical connection with the reliability of evidence or the dangers of its misuse.

5. Evidence of any relevant conduct of a party has always been admissible against him in a civil action, including relevant statements offered to prove their truth. After the hearsay rule was established, this continued to be true even when the party was incompetent to testify. Whether under modern conditions he testifies or refrains from so doing, his former statement is received as evidence of the truth of the matter stated, regardless of oath or opportunity to cross-examine and his availability or unavailability as a witness. It is easy to say that he cannot be heard to object that he was not under oath or subject to cross-examination when he made the statement, particularly when he made it as of his own knowledge. It is much less easy to understand why it is immaterial whether he is oathworthy or that he had not perceived the matter stated but was relying upon what some stranger or friend told him. When he was incompetent to testify, he had to bear the risk that the jurors would be misled. Now that he is competent, he can deny that he made the statement or explain why he said whatever he concedes having said as well as what he meant by it. But the fact remains that the statement was made without any of the usual safeguards which, if present, would enable the jurors to evaluate it as evidence of the fact stated, and the sole justification for its

use is that an inaccurate valuation will harm only the objecting adversary.

6. Where a witness who is present and subject to cross-examination verifies a statement in writing as having been made at or about the time of the matter recorded therein and swears that he then knew that the facts were as stated but now has no recollection of them, the content of the writing is obviously a previous statement by the witness or another. It is neither consistent nor inconsistent with his present testimony, because he is unable to testify from present memory. He is subject to cross-examination, but the cross-examination cannot test any element of his perception of the matter stated. It may test his general capacity for perception and his use of language, but attempts to probe his memory or to expose insincerity in making or previously verifying the writing are rarely, if ever, fruitful. Arthur Train has spoken of the practical impossibility of effective cross-examination through an interpreter, but that is a less exasperating experience, as any lawyer will testify who has tried to cross-examine a clever or cautious, to say nothing of a crooked, witness who is relying upon a memorandum of past recollection. And yet the content of such a memorandum is held admissible in almost every jurisdiction. It is true that the early courts, talking in terms of refreshment of recollection, confused this use of a memorandum as a substitute for recollection with the use of a memorandum to revive present memory. But where a court is pressed with the hearsay objection, it is likely to resort to the theory which Thayer enunciated, namely, that the witness adopts the content of the memorandum as his pres-

ent testimony because he is convinced that it contains a correct statement of what he once knew but cannot now remember. And this makes him testimonially qualified. This may be an acceptable explanation but it does not change the fact that the trier is asked to rely upon a previous unsworn and un-cross-examined statement by a witness who is not subject to effective cross-examination under oath.

In each of these six situations the evidence is such that every sensible person, seeking in the ordinary affairs of life to ascertain the state of facts which it tends to prove, would want to hear and consider, with the possible exception of an admission by a party who was prevented by some rule of law from denying having made it or from explaining it or testifying to what he did say or meant to say. Some of the rulings can be explained only as supposedly necessary concomitants of the adversary system; for some there is no rational explanation. Historical accident or a shift in emphasis from the concept of cross-examination as a protection of the adversary to cross-examination as a means of furnishing the trier with reliable data for evaluation of the evidence may account for some. In none of them, however, is any circumstance of the utterance by a nonparty treated as a reason for not requiring opportunity for cross-examination. If the doctrine applied in these situations were applied uniformly or consistently to evidence of hearsay statements by nonparties, there could be no exceptions to the hearsay rule save admissions and former testimony; those cases to which the hearsay rule has never been applied would have to be overruled or regarded as historical accidents and justified only by their antiquity.

The fact is, however, that the courts have felt called upon to explain these early exceptions, as well as some others, as rationally justified. There are at least sixteen exceptions, each supported by some respectable authority, in which unsworn, un-cross-examined statements of persons not parties to the action and not present in court are received in evidence. These are Shop Books and Regular Entries, Official Written Statements, Reputation, Pedigree, Dying Declarations, Statements against Interest, Attestations of Subscribing Witnesses, Ancient Documents, Learned Treatises, Declarations concerning Land Boundaries, Declarations of Presently Existing State of Mind, Spontaneous Declarations, Contemporaneous Declarations, Narrative Statements of Testator, Declarations of Voter, and Vicarious Admissions.

*Conclusion* It is useless to contend that the adversary is given the same sort of protection in all these. It is likewise futile to contend that Admissions Including Confessions and Admissible Reported Testimony are not hearsay, and that in all other exceptions, there is a real guaranty of trustworthiness which serves the purpose of full protection to the adversary. In none of these sixteen is there anything in the circumstances in which the statements were made or in the content of the statements which could serve in any degree as a substitute for cross-examination. In some of them there appears to be a substitute for the oath—a factor which would create a desire to tell the truth, in many of them merely absence of a motive to falsify. This is to say that the opportunity for cross-examination is disregarded and the sole emphasis is upon the likelihood that the trier can put upon the evidence approximately the value which it deserves as tending to prove the matter in issue.

There is, therefore, no single theory or principle which will lend any element of consistency to the decisions governing hearsay and its exceptions. The whole subject needs reconsideration. The Uniform Law Commissioners have issued a proposed set of rules, which have been approved by the American Bar Association and the American Law Institute. They do much toward making the rule and its exceptions more nearly consistent and more effective as means for a practical rational solution of issues of fact. They deserve study with a view to action by both Bench and Bar.

# HEARSAY: THE RULE IN THEORY AND PRACTICE

THE THEORY of the hearsay rule is not difficult to discover, and the reasons given for its creation and persistence are reiterated in decision after decision, as demonstrated in the preceding essay. I shall recapitulate these first, briefly. What of the practice? Is there any general principle which will harmonize the decisions and make the rule in application a reasonably effective device for producing a rational resolution of disputed propositions of fact? In attempting to answer this query, I shall have to make what I fear you will find a tiresome analysis of the authorities.

## HEARSAY RULE IN THEORY

*Reasons for the Rule* As an examination of the early cases and of the opinions of early commentators demonstrates, the reasons which caused the courts to establish the rule excluding hearsay were (1) that the hearsay was not uttered under the sanction of an oath and (2) that the party against whom it was offered had had no opportunity to cross-examine. To these the judges of the nineteenth century added the incapacity of jurors to assign to hearsay its proper probative value. Today these three reasons are recognized as controlling, though some subordinate considerations are occasionally mentioned and current opinions put chief emphasis upon lack of opportunity to cross-examine.[1] Obviously these reasons rest upon the hypothesis that the utterer of the hearsay, whom we call the declarant, is the real witness; he it is who furnishes the trier the information by the use of which the issue is to be resolved. The person who appears upon the witness stand and reports the hearsay, or the writing containing it which is exhibited in court, is nothing more than the conduit through which the information is transmitted to the trier. Consequently the hearsay rule is applicable wherever the conduct of the declarant is to be used as testimony, that is, for a purpose which requires the trier to treat the declarant as if he were a witness making statements to the trier.

In this connection it must be noted that the party against whom a witness testifies is under no obligation to cross-examine, and may waive the requirement of the oath or its equivalent. Furthermore, inadmissible hearsay evidence received without objection may properly be used by the trier of fact like other evidence. Consequently, the rule excluding hearsay is erected not to protect the trier from mistake or even to lighten the burden of evaluating the evidence, but to relieve the adversary from the risk that the trier will be misled.

The oath, even when most solemnly administered, serves only as a subjective stimulus to the witness to tell what he honestly believes to be the truth. Cross-examination, intelligently conducted, will disclose all data helpful to the trier in determining (1) what information the witness intends to convey to the trier by the language he uses; (2) the belief of the witness in the truth of his testimony, that

[1] See History and Theory of the Hearsay Rule, pp. 106–40 *supra*.

is, his sincerity; (3) the extent to which what the witness purports to remember is the product of memory or of some other mental process such as reconstruction or the mistaken adoption as his own of the experience of another; and (4) the extent to which what the witness testifies that he perceived corresponds to what was then and there open to his observation or capable of being perceived. Any one of these may be of controlling importance or of no importance in a particular case. For example, when the witness testifies to a past perception of objective matter, all of them will be essential. When he testifies to his then existing subjective condition, his memory is not involved; the danger of mistake in perception is negligible; and though there may be some necessity for clarification of his language, the chief risk lies in reliance on his good faith. Because the subject matter is so peculiarly within his own knowledge, his sincerity or lack of it is of paramount importance. But when the evidence is offered as tending to prove the truth of declarant's statement, the courts and most modern commentators classify it as hearsay, whether the risk or danger be single or multiple.

### HEARSAY RULE IN PRACTICE

*In Practice* Thus far, the courts have had little or no difficulty in dealing with specific situations. But once this line is passed, confusion begins.

*Need Not Be a Communication* Of course, a statement is none the less hearsay because it was not intended as a communication. Though spoken in a soliloquy or in a prayer when the declarant believed himself safely isolated from all hearers, or written in a secret diary kept under lock and key, if offered in evidence as tending to prove the truth of the matter asserted, the proponent is asking the trier to treat the declarant in all respects as if he were making it as a communication on the witness stand.

*Nonverbal Communication* It is a commonplace that nonverbal conduct may be and often is used as a substitute for words in making a communication. Thus, where a child, who had been molested by an adult, was asked whether the man who had had him in the park was among a group of men in the police station, and the child pointed at a Mr. Johnson, his pointing was clearly a substitute for the words, "He is the man." Yet a Wisconsin court, with an obtuseness rarely found in a judicial opinion, solemnly declared that the policeman's testimony describing the incident was not hearsay evidence, that he was testifying to something he saw, something the boy did in his presence. He was relying on what he observed and not on what the boy told him.[2]

Ordinarily the mere fact that a communication occurred between A and B, and that certain conduct of B followed the conversation, would have no trace of hearsay in it. But if evidence of B's conduct is offered as tending to show the content and truth of matter asserted in the conversation, the hearsay element does exist. Thus, if a witness testifies that he saw a small child at the scene of a homicide,

[2] Johnson v. State, 254 Wis. 320, 36 N.W.2d 86 (1949).

had a conversation with him, and then went into the neighboring woods and found incriminating articles later shown to belong to the defendant, there is no element of hearsay involved in the evidence unless it is offered to induce the trier to believe that the child had revealed to W information that incriminated the defendant to a greater degree than did mere proof of his ownership of the articles. If the witness had testified that after the conversation he went into the woods "the way the child pointed to look for the clothes and the gun," he would in effect have been saying that the child had told him that defendant had gone that way with the clothes and the gun. And so the South Carolina Supreme Court held, reversing a contrary ruling by the trial judge.[3] In many cases the circumstances make it clear that the nonverbal conduct was intended to operate as an assertion. In others they leave the conduct ambiguous. For example, if after a crime has been committed X flees, he may be doing so in order to cast suspicion upon himself and divert it from the real culprit. If so, he is using flight as a substitute for words equivalent to a confession of guilt. If X is not the party against whom the evidence is offered the courts usually exclude it as hearsay, declaring the flight to be the equivalent of a confession of guilt, a declaration against penal interest. This obviously resolves the ambiguity against the proponent by assuming X's purpose to be to draw suspicion upon himself, and his conduct to be intended as a communication; but the courts have not made clear this process of analysis.

[3] State v. Bealin, 201 S.C. 490, 23 S.E.2d 746 (1943).

*Verbal Conduct* Two situations where verbal conduct is offered in evidence to prove the truth of the matter therein asserted have caused sharp conflict, namely, statements by a party and those made in former testimony.

1. *Personal admissions.*—It is difficult to see why the hearsay quality of evidence can be altered by the fact that the declarant is a party to the action, even where the evidence is offered against him. And most commentators have classified it as hearsay. But the greatest of American commentators have put personal admissions in a nonhearsay category. Greenleaf, who in 1842 gave the profession the first comprehensive American treatise on evidence, observed that they were commonly designated as admissions against interest though in fact they frequently had no such quality when made. He declared that an admission is "more properly admissible as a substitute for the ordinary and legal proof." Wharton in 1877 paraphrased this dictum by classifying an admission as "a fact to be proved, not evidence to prove a fact." Greenleaf's text remained without challenge through the first fifteen editions. Neither Greenleaf nor any of his disciples seems to have realized the practical significance of this doctrine. It put extrajudicial admissions upon the same basis as solemn judicial admissions. The only question for the trier of fact on this theory is whether the admission was made; if so, it is conclusive. Greenleaf purported to be adopting the view of Mascardus in his treatise on the Roman law which was published 1584–88. Greenleaf, of course, knew that the Roman law had no rule excluding hearsay; it dealt not with admissibility but with weight of evidence. He must have known

also that in the sixteenth century the common law did not exclude hearsay, and, further, it is difficult to believe that he was not aware that Mascardus distinguished sharply between extrajudicial and judicial admissions and rated the former as of slight value unless corroborated.

Apparently the great Thayer expressed no dissent from the view of Greenleaf, but it was to be expected that when in the sixteenth edition of Greenleaf, Wigmore undertook to revise the text covering the general principles of the subject, he would critically reexamine this theory. He exposed the error of treating an extrajudicial admission as the equivalent of a judicial admission, but he insisted that Greenleaf was right in not classifying an admission as an exception to the hearsay rule, receivable for the truth of the matter asserted in it. He declared it receivable only as a statement contradictory to the position which the admitter was taking at the trial; its sole effect was to weaken or destroy that position; it was like a prior contradictory statement of a witness; it could never be used as positive evidence of the fact stated. For this contention he had no appreciable support in the judicial decisions. He repeated it, however, in the first edition of his master work, but abandoned it in his second edition.[4] He conceded, as is now universally held, that an admission is receivable as evidence of the truth of the matter asserted. But he apparently did not regard it as hearsay, though it falls squarely within his description of hearsay, as an extrajudicial assertion offered to prove the truth of the

[4] See 4 WIGMORE, EVIDENCE §§1048 *et seq.* (3d ed. 1940); Morgan, *Admissions as an Exception to the Hearsay Rule*, 30 YALE L.J. 355 (1921).

matter asserted. Attempts by some of his disciples to support his position, by proving that an admission is merely circumstantial evidence of the truth of the assertion, rest upon the analysis that an inference may properly be drawn from the utterance to a belief in the truth of the matter stated, and from that belief to the fact which created the belief.[5] This requires reliance upon the asserter's use of language, his sincerity, memory, and perception. This is to say, it requires the trier to treat the admitter as if he were, for all purposes, a witness. For the trier, in order to give testimony its proper value, must consciously or unconsciously use exactly this same series of inferences in dealing with every statement made by a witness on the stand. To be sure, the theory upon which the admission is received for the truth of the matter asserted has little or no importance to the practitioner. But it is of importance to one seeking to find the principles upon which a sensible, consistent body of law governing the admissibility of evidence should be based.

2. *Reported testimony.*—Evidence of statements made in former testimony in a judicial proceeding is generally treated as hearsay. Wigmore disagrees[6] as to so much of such evidence as is receivable, but he does not attempt to explain the rejection of the remainder of this class of evidence on any other ground than its violation of the hearsay rule. So much of it as is admitted he puts in the same class as depositions, taken pursuant to statute, for use in the case in question. It is too obvious for argument

[5] See Strahorn, *A Reconsideration of the Hearsay Rule and Admissions*, 85 U. PA. L. REV. 484, 564 (1937).

[6] 5 WIGMORE, EVIDENCE §1370 (3d ed. 1940).

that there are important distinctions between the two, which make his discussion and his citations less persuasive than usual. But, here again, whether the admissible evidence is an exception to the hearsay rule or merely an example of a situation to which it is not applicable is of only theoretical importance. The fact remains that a statement made by one who is not now present and subject to cross-examination is received in evidence for the truth of the matter stated.

*Presence or Absence of Hearsay Dangers* In all the foregoing the reception of the evidence makes the declarant in truth the witness to the matter declared. What of evidence of an utterance offered for a purpose other than as tending to prove the truth of the matter stated? One or more or none of the four risks or dangers of error in testimony may be present. For example, none is involved where the words have operative effect regardless of the meaning which the declarant intended them to have, as where evidence of the exchange of words is offered to prove an offer and its acceptance in a jurisdiction accepting the objective theory of contracts. Similarly, evidence of words uttered in the presence of a person is relevant upon the issue whether he heard them. What was said may be an operative fact or may be only so-called circumstantial evidence of an operative fact, such as the speaker's or hearer's good faith or due diligence or due care. The speaker is in no sense a witness to the truth of the matter stated. Neither the opponent of the evidence nor the trier is subjected to any of the risks or dangers inherent in hearsay.

But when the evidence is to be used for a purpose which does make him bear one or more of the risks, which one or what combination of two or more is or should be the criterion for classification as hearsay or nonhearsay?

*Sincerity and Use of Language* Suppose that evidence of declarant's words is offered to prove that they meant to him what they would have meant to the ordinary person and that he had the knowledge of the matter which the words would have conveyed to the ordinary person. Some of the hearsay dangers are obviously present. The declarant's use of language may be unusual. Every practicing lawyer who has had to deal with an illiterate or an expert, either as a client or as a witness, must have had this truth impressed upon him. And where there is a communication between third persons, they may have been using a special code, which gave impossible, artificial meanings to the ordinary words used therein, such as "buy" to mean "sell," or "hold" to mean "release." There are numerous current cases in which a defendant is charged with possessing or conducting a place for the making or registering of bets on specified sporting events, and in which a policeman testifies that while in the place he answered the telephone on several occasions within a specified period and on each occasion heard through the receiver the voice of a person who identified himself only by initials and used language which in race track jargon meant a request to register a bet or bets on one or more of the horse races scheduled for the day. There was nothing to show the identity of the speaker or the meaning which he attached to the words. The mere use of the jargon is, of course, relevant as tending to show that it was used in its customary meaning, but it was essential for the trier to determine whether the declarant was using this jargon as a code to cover some transaction other than a bet on a sporting event. And it was of crucial importance to determine whether the declarant was sincere, that is, whether he was, for example, a so-called stool pigeon or a person who was attempting to cause a false accusation of defendant, or whether he was actually requesting the registration of a bet. The courts, however, have had no hesitation in declaring the evidence nonhearsay, treating the words as an actual request to register a bet and not as mere evidence that they were used in the customary sense. And they do not even discuss the element of sincerity.[7]

This latter element is likewise entirely disregarded in cases where to prove declarant's knowledge of a matter which is otherwise established, evidence of his assertion concerning the matter is offered. Thus, as tending to prove that the conductor of a train knew that the engineer was drunk before the train started, evidence is offered of the conductor's statement to a passenger boarding the train, "Be careful, the engineer is drunk." The courts universally treat this sort of evidence as nonhearsay,[8] though it is obvious that unless the declarant had seen the engineer or had been informed of his condition by others, he had

[7] See, e.g., Commonwealth v. Jensky, 318 Mass. 350, 61 N.E.2d 532 (1945).

[8] See, e.g., Pruett v. Caldwell & N.R. Co., 141 N.C. 332, 53 S.E. 852 (1906); 2 WIGMORE, EVIDENCE §§266, 266a (3d ed. 1940); 6 *id.* §1790 (1940).

no knowledge of the fact, and may have been joking or drawing a conclusion from his previous knowledge of the habits of the engineer.

*Sincerity and Memory* In addition, the risk of inaccurate memory may be present. Numerous decisions deal with a declarant's utterance used to prove his then existing belief where that belief is to be made the basis for an inference that he had the same belief at a previous time when a material event happened. For example, a grantor declares that for specified reasons he will have to make a new plan for disposing of his property among named persons to whom he has previously handed deeds of conveyance. Evidence of the declaration is offered as tending to prove his belief that he still owns the property, from which it may be inferred that when he handed the deeds to the respective grantees, he did not intend them to be effective as conveyances.[9] This requires the trier to rely upon the sincerity of declarant's original statement and upon the accuracy of his memory as to his state of mind at the time of the previous transaction. In like manner, a testator declares that he has in his will left all his property to X. The undisputed fact is that the duly executed will leaves all the property to Y. Evidence of the testator's declaration is offered to prove that at the time of his statement he believed that his will disposed of all his property to X, from which it is to be inferred that he had the same belief at the time of the execution of the will, and, there-

[9] Mower v. Mower, 64 Utah 260, 228 Pac. 911 (1924); Whitlow v. Durst, 20 Cal.2d 523, 127 P.2d 530 (1942).

fore, did not understand what he was doing.[10] Here again the original statement has no value unless declarant was sincere in making it, and the deduction to his belief at the time of execution assumes the accuracy of his memory. The same theory is applied by most courts in will contests where the issue is revocation or undue influence.[11] Evidence of a testator's statements that the will exists or has been revoked or has been executed because of specified coercive conduct of interested third persons is received to prove a past state of mind, namely, the *animus revocandi* or lack of it or susceptibility to undue influence. Notwithstanding the obvious risks affecting both sincerity and memory, the courts are in general agreement in declaring the evidence nonhearsay.

To receive an utterance as circumstantial evidence of the declarant's presently existing state of mind will not carry any greater risk of insincerity than to receive as direct evidence an express assertion of that state of mind under similar circumstances. And it is now rather well settled that evidence of a statement of a presently existing state of mind, or emotion, or other subjective condition offered to prove the matter stated is receivable as an exception to the hearsay rule.

*Inferences to Future Conduct* It will be noted that the state of mind of a declarant at the moment of the utterance is rarely of legal significance except as a basis of inference to his state of mind at some earlier or later time. The infer-

[10] Waterman v. Whitney, 11 N.Y. 157 (1854).
[11] See cases in 79 A.L.R. 1427, 1447; *id.* 1488, 1493 (1932); 172 *id.* 344, 354 (1948).

ence which a trier may draw from the fact that a person had a specified state of mind or emotion at the time he exhibited certain conduct does not depend upon the kind of evidence which induced the trier to find the existence of that state: if the evidence was admissible and had the requisite probative value, it matters not whether it was hearsay or nonhearsay. If the fact to be inferred is the existence of another state of mind or emotion and the persistence for a reasonable time of either or both states, the process of inference will require no additional reliance upon that person's use of language or sincerity or memory or perception. Persistence of a mental condition may have some quality akin to memory but it carries no risk of reconstruction or of unconscious adoption of another's experience. Where the state of mind is intent or purpose or plan to do a specified act, and it is shown that that act has been done, the further inference is justified that he who had that state of mind is more likely to have done the act than anyone who had no such state of mind. And this process likewise involves no additional hearsay danger. The judicial opinions are consistent with these conclusions.[12]

*Inference to Past Conduct* It is when the earlier state of mind or emotion found by inference from the existing state of mind is to be used as a basis for an inference to an objective matter which created that state of mind or emotion that the hearsay problem receives serious judicial

[12] See discussion and citations in McCormick, Evidence, §270 (1954).

consideration. The clearest illustrations are found in the cases involving a testator's statements. For example, if a testator asserts that he has revoked a specified will, evidence of his assertion, as previously noted, will be received as tending to prove that at the time of the assertion he believed the will to be no longer effective, which includes a belief that at some earlier time it became ineffective. From this belief, if found by the trier, may be inferred the belief that at that earlier time he intended to make the will ineffective, that is, that he then had the *animus revocandi.* But the process must stop here. There can be no inference that the *animus revocandi,* the intent to revoke, existed some time, no matter how short, before that specified earlier time, so as to transform it into an intent or plan to do the intended act and thus bring it into the class of declarations of intent to be used as a basis for an inference to future action, declarations which fall within a recognized exception to the hearsay rule. For such a process would obviously make the evidence receivable for the truth of the matter asserted in it, and this by hypothesis is forbidden by the accepted doctrine. Nor can the testator's belief that he has revoked the will be used as the basis for an inference to his belief that he has done or caused to be done the requisite revoking acts, for example, mutilation or destruction of the document, even where the mutilation or destruction is conceded or is established by other evidence. This process also would in effect make the evidence admissible for the truth of the matter asserted.

Now consider the situation where the conduct which the proponent offers to prove is not an assertion of the truth of any proposition which declarant had consciously in mind when the assertion was made. The most thoroughly considered case is *Wright v. Tatham*,[13] which was exhaustively argued by distinguished counsel before distinguished judges in the Exchequer Chamber and the House of Lords. There, several letters written by persons since deceased to a testator were offered in evidence as tending to show the belief of the respective writers that the testator was sane. No statement in any letter even mentioned or referred to the testator's mental condition, but the content of each letter was such as to justify the inference that its writer believed him to be sane. Some of the judges pointed out, and all of them apparently agreed, that the testimony of a witness in open court as to his opinion of the sanity or insanity of a testator was merely a "compendious mode" of stating "the result of the actual observation of the witness from acts done, as to the habits and demeanor" of the testator. Consequently, the proponents were seeking to have each letter used as the equivalent of an assertion by the writer that the objective conduct of the testator observed by the writer was that of a sane man, and the letter was subject to objection as hearsay. It is clear that the state of mind of each writer was, of itself, irrelevant as evidence of the state of mind of the testator; it became relevant only if it was to be used as a basis for an inference to the facts which produced the state of mind. Assuming that the letter by its content reflected the actual state of mind of the writer, that is, assuming his sincerity, since it was written some time after the testator's actions were

[13] 5 Cl. & Fin. 670 (House of Lords 1838); same case in Exchequer Chamber, 7 A. & E. 313 (1837).

open to the writer's observation, the writer's memory was involved; the crucial element, however, concerned the adequacy and accuracy of his observation. And the conduct observed was not that of the writer himself but of another. The decision of the judges was based on objections applicable to both opinion evidence and hearsay evidence.

In 1914 a case came before the House of Lords which involved substantially the same hearsay problem.[14] It had been badly bungled in the courts below by both counsel and judges by treating the evidence as involving only the exception for declarations against interest,[15] so that the decisive question came before the Lords without the benefit of previous judicial decision rendered after careful analysis and debate by counsel. The issue was whether a child born to Alice Lloyd after the death of a workman, Whittall, was entitled to compensation as Whittall's child. This required proof that Whittall was the father and intended to support the child. Although the Court of Appeal stated specifically that the questioned evidence was tendered to prove Whittall's intention to support the child, and assumed that the trial judge's finding of paternity was supported by other evidence, all of the opinions, except that of Lord Moulton in the House of Lords, discuss the admissibility of the evidence of Whittall's statements upon the issue of paternity. These were made after he had full knowledge that Miss Lloyd was pregnant and included an agreement to marry her, and statements of an intent to marry her and of a desire to work as much as he could in order to provide a home for himself and her. There was no express declara-

[14] Lloyd v. Powell Duffryn Steam Coal Company, Limited, L.R. [1914] App. Cas. 733.

[15] L.R. [1913] 2 K.B. 130.

tion that he was the father of the child, but some of the judges viewed the statements as acknowledgments of paternity. They could have reached this view only by a process of inference from the state of mind which Whittall's conduct indicated.

As Lord Moulton pointed out, evidence of a man's state of mind may consist of relevant nonverbal acts, or of words. And though he seemed to consider an express declaration of intent nonhearsay even when offered to prove the truth of the declaration, he confined his consideration to admissibility of Whittall's statements on the issue of intent to support, and held it unnecessary to go further. As to the issue of paternity, it must be clear that Whittall's agreement to marry Miss Lloyd and his statements of intent and desire are relevant only as evidence of belief that he was the father of her unborn child; this, so far as matters within his knowledge were concerned, included the belief that he had had intercourse with her during the period of conception, which was some five months before the statements were made. He could have had this belief, on the theory on which the evidence was offered, only if he was sincere in entering into the agreement and in making the statements. The accuracy of his belief depended upon the accuracy of his memory and of his perception. Consequently, most of the hearsay dangers were present, but the subject matter of the memory and perception was the declarant's own conduct of a kind in which the risks of mistake were negligible. Technically, his belief that he was the father involved matter of which he could have had no personal knowledge, as the Court of Appeal took care to point out, namely, that the mother had had no intercourse with another man during the possible period of conception. In this view the opinion rule as well as the hearsay rule presented the same sort of barrier as in the Tatham case. So far as the reported opinions show, that case was never mentioned. The Law Lords paid no attention to it, and certainly no one concerned with the appeal took the trouble to analyze the evidence as amounting to unsworn, un-cross-examined assertions concerning Whittall's past experiences. But three of the four Law Lords had no doubt of its admissibility on the issue of paternity as well as on the issue of intent to support.

A New York case presents a somewhat similar problem. As tending to prove the condition of a patient, evidence was offered that the treatment given or prescribed by a competent physician was the standard treatment for a specified condition. It was held objectionable as hearsay.[16] The situation differs from that in *Wright v. Tatham* in that the doctor's state of mind was specifically concerned with the matter perceived by him.

Upon analysis the hearsay dangers are obvious. By the examination the physician perceived the symptoms of the patient. When he decided that a prescribed treatment was suitable, he had definitely determined that the symptoms were those of a particular ailment, and, it is believed, had put his thought to himself in words as clearly as if he had expressed it in a soliloquy. If so, evidence of the treatment offered as tending to prove that the patient's symptoms

[16] Thompson v. Manhattan Ry. Co., 11 App. Div. 182, 42 N.Y.S. 896 (1896). But *cf.* Phoenix Refining Co. v. Walker, 108 S.W.2d 323 (Tex. Civ. App. 1937).

were those of the specified ailment is the equivalent of evidence of an assertion by the doctor of the observed symptoms. The trier was put to the same task in valuing the evidence as if it were evidence of an entry in the doctor's diary, made contemporaneously with or shortly after the examination, stating that the symptoms of the patient indicated ailment X.

The question often requires an answer where evidence of silence or inaction is offered as tending to prove an external event or condition. The decisions are in confusion. Few of them are thoroughly considered. In many of them, the evidence is rejected as irrelevant without discussion. In some others the relevancy is assumed but there is no analysis of the process by which the proving fact has any value as evidence of the fact to be proved. For example, in a Minnesota case,[17] plaintiff testified that she and other standing passengers on defendant's streetcar were hurled to the floor by the violent jerk of the car caused by its sudden stopping. Defendant offered to prove that no claim for injury on that account had been made by any passenger other than the plaintiff. The evidence was received over objection, and the opinion affirming this ruling does not indicate that any hearsay problem was involved. In a number of cases, however, the objection is made that the silence or inaction amounts to a statement of an objective fact, and that the evidence is hearsay.[18] Thus the North Carolina Supreme Court held inadmissible as hearsay testimony by members of a family that the mother had never mentioned

[17] Sullivan v. Minneapolis Street Railway, 161 Minn. 45, 200 N.W. 922 (1924).

[18] See excellent article by Falknor, *Silence as Hearsay*, 89 U. Pa. L. Rev. 192 (1940).

having been served with a summons when that was offered to prove that she had not been served.[19] On the other hand, a Court of Appeals in Texas held relevant and admissible as nonhearsay the testimony of members of a family that another member had never mentioned an alleged trust of which he was a beneficiary, offered as tending to prove that there was no such trust.[20]

In Massachusetts, a number of cases admit evidence of failure to complain as to the quality of an article of food or other merchandise as tending to prove its quality as expressly or impliedly warranted, without considering any factor affecting admissibility[21] except relevancy, while a New Hampshire court and a New York court exclude the evidence as hearsay.[22] In *Shepard v. United States,*[23] Mr. Justice Cardozo warned that to permit such inferences to past conduct cut deeply into the hearsay rule.

The conclusion to be drawn from this line of decisions seems to be this: Evidence of conduct of a declarant other than an assertion that he perceived a matter will not be recognized as hearsay unless the court is convinced that the conduct is relevant only as a basis for an inference that he did perceive the matter. And the task of convincing the court requires unusually careful preparation on evi-

[19] Lake Drainage Comm'rs v. Spencer, 174 N.C. 36, 93 S.E. 435 (1917), and see Note 24 N.C. L. Rev. 274 (1946).

[20] Latham v. Houston Land & Trust Co., 62 S.W. 2d 519 (Tex. Civ. App. 1933).

[21] See, e.g., Landfield v. Albiani Lunch Co., 268 Mass. 528, 168 N.E. 160 (1929).

[22] Menard v. Cashman, 94 N.H. 428, 55 A.2d 156 (1947); James K. Thompson Co., Inc. v. International Compositions Co., 191 App. Div. 553, 181 N.Y.S. 637 (1920); Altkrug v. William Whitman Co., Inc. 185 App. Div. 744, 173 N.Y.S. 669 (1919).

[23] 290 U.S. 96, 54 S. Ct. 22 (1933).

dential problems. Rarely does counsel make a pretrial examination of the evidence expected to be offered by him or by his adversary to discover hearsay elements that may be hidden in it. The reported cases demonstrate that the hearsay quality of such evidence does not leap to the consciousness. It is frequently undiscerned by counsel and court. The requisite analysis is often difficult to make and more difficult to expound. The exposition must in the first instance be made to the trial judge, who must rule promptly and without previous opportunity for study. Press of business makes unduly costly the delay required for extended argument upon the admissibility of evidence. And it is only where the problem and counsel's position with reference to it has been fairly presented at the trial that the judge's ruling will be seriously considered by the appellate court.

It is therefore submitted that the foregoing survey of the decisions shows the practical futility of expecting or requiring such difficult analysis in everyday practice, and demonstrates the wisdom of the Uniform Commissioners in classifying as hearsay statements only those offered in evidence as tending to prove the truth of the matter stated. All other relevant conduct of a person, evidence of which is offered, is not subject to objection as hearsay regardless of whether reception of the evidence involves one or more of the dangers which might be lessened or eliminated by cross-examination.

*Considerations Determinative of Admissibility* If this conclusion is accepted, if the presence of the dangers which oath and cross-examination are deemed potent to render negligible does not condemn the evidence as hearsay, the question naturally arises to what extent does the presence or absence of these safeguards, or some adequate substitute for them, determine the admissibility of evidence which the court regards as unquestionable hearsay. Previously, I have pointed out (1) that evidence of prior statements made by a witness now testifying under oath and subject to cross-examination, whether consistent or inconsistent with his present testimony, is inadmissible; (2) that even though the prior statement was made in a judicial proceeding under oath and subjected to cross-examination by the very party against whom it is now offered, the evidence is excluded. The fact that it was previously subject to cross-examination under oath and is, when the evidence is offered, subject to a second cross-examination under oath, does not validate it; and (3) that if the statement was spontaneous concerning an exciting event which caused it to be made, the evidence is receivable, not because the declarant is now under oath and subject to cross-examination, but because the statement was made under circumstances indicating not a motive to tell the truth but lack of motive and opportunity to deceive. Full opportunity for cross-examination under oath therefore, does not prevent classification as inadmissible hearsay.

What of the numerous situations where concededly hearsay evidence—evidence of statements made by declarant not under oath or subject to cross-examination when made or when the evidence is offered—is admitted? Consider some half a dozen of them most commonly encountered.

1. *Dying declarations.*—Disregard for the moment the

arbitrary limitations upon admissibility to prosecutions for the homicide of the declarant. The realization of speedily impending death is accepted as a substitute for the oath. The earlier opinions stress declarant's belief in future rewards and punishments: No one "who is immediately going into the presence of his Maker will do so with a lie on his lips." But the current view is that even his blatant irreverence goes only to the weight of the evidence and absence of a belief in divine punishment does not require exclusion. The stimulus to truth-telling may be strong or weak. Still there is nothing approaching the safeguards of cross-examination, which are greatly needed in view of the assumed mental condition of the declarant.

2. *Declarations against interest.*—Two theories have been advanced by the courts: (*a*) that no person will concede even to himself the existence of a fact which will subject him to pecuniary liability or injure or destroy his interest in property unless he believes that the fact exists; (*b*) that no person will manufacture false evidence against himself. Here again we may disregard the inconsistencies in the application of the rule which negate the reasons on which it is said to be based. Self-interest may furnish a stimulus equal to that of an oath. But we look in vain for any equivalent of opportunity to cross-examine. What check is there of completeness in perception or in narration, or of accuracy of memory?

3. *Official written statements.*—Here the duty to observe and record correctly is thought to serve the function of the oath. The dangers of mistake in perception or memory are usually slight. The English cases require that the writings

be open to public inspection as an additional safeguard, thus implying that dangers do exist which interested persons should have the opportunity to discover and have corrected. Knowledge of the likelihood of discovery also adds to the effectiveness of the stimulus to truth-telling. There is obviously nothing to take the place of cross-examination as to sincerity or the care taken in observation by the declarant.

4. *Business entries.*—Many of the considerations applicable to official statements are pertinent here, particularly when the entry is made in the course of business. The original entries are usually highly self-serving, and for this reason the English common law courts rejected them, except when by the exercise of mental gymnastics an entry of payment could be regarded as transforming them into declarations against interest. Consequently, there is no positive stimulus to make a correct charging entry except a realization that errors are likely to be discovered by the customer. There is the force of routine and habit which makes it more troublesome to falsify than to record accurately, but there is no equivalent of opportunity to cross-examine even by the party against whom the charge is made. And it must be remembered that the entry, whenever it is relevant, is admitted against a complete stranger who has had no reason or opportunity to question its accuracy when made.

5. *Spontaneous statements.*—Declarations describing or explaining an exciting event made by a declarant who perceived the event while in the stress of a nervous excitement caused by the event are spontaneous statements. Spon-

taneity negatives desire or opportunity to fabricate but it can hardly serve as a positive stimulus to speak truly. Furthermore, the excitement tends to make both perception and narration less than usually accurate. Consequently the substitute for the oath is not an adequate sanction, and the safeguards provided by cross-examination are totally lacking.

6. *Pedigree declarations.*—Statements of a person since deceased who is shown to have been related by blood or marriage to the person concerning whose relationship he made the statement are pedigree declarations. The relationship is said to be sufficient to establish knowledge of the fact stated either by personal observation or through family tradition. The statement must have been made before controversy and without motive to falsify. It is too clear for argument that there is no adequate substitute for the oath. A mere absence of a motive to falsify is all that is required. And there is not even the remotest equivalent of cross-examination as to use of language, memory or perception. Yet this is one of the oldest exceptions to the hearsay rule, and evidence of this sort is in constant use in trial courts, though the cases currently reaching the appellate tribunal are few.

This wearisome review of the authorities seems to me to constitute a clear demonstration that our modern courts in dealing with hearsay, while giving lip service to the reasons which impelled their predecessors to create the rule, have in fact entirely disregarded them. The oath and opportunity for cross-examination, and even oath and actual cross-examination do not save the utterance from exclusion as hearsay; the absence of both does not require its exclusion. The decisions indicate a realization that emphasis upon the theoretical value of oath and cross-examination as instruments for the discovery of truth (*a*) has obscured the limits of their value in day-to-day practice in ordinary litigation, and (*b*) has created an entirely unrealistic assumption of naive credulity of jurors and their incapacity to evaluate hearsay as distinguished from first-hand testimony. The test of admissibility which seems to me to be applied in most of the exceptions is this: "Is the evidence offered of such a quality that a trier of fact, and particularly a modern jury, could put upon it a reasonably accurate value as tending to prove the truth of the proposition which it is offered to prove?" The refusal of the courts to abandon the orthodox statements as to the reasons for excluding hearsay and their purporting to find some adequate substitute for oath and cross-examination in evidence which they believe well worth consideration by any intelligent trier of fact may make the law as to hearsay seem rational and consistent. But it is only a seeming. It may make plausible Wigmore's thesis that the law is in this respect fundamentally sound. In support of it he first eliminates from the hearsay category admissions and former testimony, and in this process includes vicarious admissions of all kinds, which in many instances are hearsay by any test. Then he purports to find in each exception to the rule (1) a so-called guaranty of trustworthiness which takes the place of the oath (if not of oath and cross-examination) and (2) some necessity for not insisting upon direct testimony by the declarant. An examination of the cases, however, shows no guaranty which would be even a weak substitute for cross-examination and in many instances the so-called substitute for the oath is merely an absence of a motive to falsify, not a stimulus to tell the truth. And the so-called necessity varies from actual inability to secure declarant's presence to mere inconvenience or to the supposedly slight value which would be added to the evidence by oath and cross-examination.

My submission is that Wigmore has rendered no service to the profession by such a classification, and thereby has, much against his own desires and convictions, encouraged piecemeal rather than fundamental reform. I realize that the Bar, and perhaps the Bench, are not prepared for radical reform which would make admissible all hearsay that a court considers as having appreciable value. Experience with the Model Code of the American Law Institute is conclusive on that. The Uniform Rules of Evidence, lately approved by the Institute and by the American Bar Association are much less radical. Their adoption would make the rules governing hearsay reflect in general the reasons which appear to govern the current attitude of the more liberal courts. They call for serious consideration by the profession, if we really want to make a trial a rational proceeding for the discovery of the facts affecting the rights and duties of the litigants. Will the usual inertia of the Bar make them only another neglected proposal of so-called dreamers?

# HEARSAY: THE RULE IN CONJUNCTION WITH OTHER EXCLUSIONARY RULES

THE EFFECT of the exclusionary rules of evidence in combination is rarely, if ever, the subject of judicial discussion. The usual judicial precedent deals with the application of one or two of the recognized rules in isolation. The proposition debated is whether the evidence falls within the rule, not whether its application will or will not produce a sensible result or whether the evidence has greater persuasive force and more obvious indicia of verity than other evidence unquestionably admissible and actually received in the case. At times a court is influenced to create a qualification of an established rule in a situation where its application would work a startling injustice, or a legislature will grant relief by modifying or repealing an ancient rule, when experience of judges and counsel has demonstrated the needless obstruction to fair and orderly presentation of the facts caused by its enforcement in a modern setting. The lawyer in active practice, the busy trial judge, the appellate court which only occasionally has to solve a troublesome procedural problem have neither time nor occasion to survey the field as a whole, or to inquire what, if any, reason is the basis for a particular rule, or whether the application of that reason would explain, strengthen, or destroy another accepted rule. Each deals with the specific problem presented, and only rarely will a court of last resort expressly declare an established rule outmoded. The usual response to dissatisfied counsel and litigants is the advice that reform is the function of the legislature. Even the great commentators, Greenleaf, Thayer, and Wigmore, do not demonstrate the need for reconsideration of the entire subject by contrasting the reasoning in one segment with that in another. When a law professor points out that if the recognized master of the subject requires nine volumes of text to expound the principles and rules applicable to proof of the merits of a properly pleaded cause or defense, there must be something wrong somewhere, he is usually met by sarcastic remarks concerning the verbosity of academic theorists and the avarice of law book publishers. And if he discusses a single pertinent hypothetical case in which the proffered evidence involves problems of incompetence and privileges of witnesses and of admissibility of testimony from competent unprivileged sources, the remarks are directed to the capacity of a fertile imagination to invent the practically impossible. I shall take the risk of being the target of such remarks, insisting, however, that my only unlikely supposition involves the unavailability of two declarants, for each problem that I shall discuss has been presented in actual litigation, and I shall treat each first as an isolated problem before contrasting the result of its solution with that in each of the others.

Mr. Pedestrian was run down at or near a street crossing by an automobile driven by chauffeur Benjamin Blunt, employed by the defendant, Oliver Owner. The accident was witnessed by two men, Walter Warren and William Watson, who immediately rushed to Pedestrian's aid. Warren called loudly for a policeman and Watson hurried away to summon an ambulance. Policeman Vaughn came to the scene within two or three minutes and Warren told him what he had seen. Pedestrian was taken to a hospital. In the afternoon of the same day, some four or five hours after the accident, Warren dictated to Gore, a notary public, a detailed account of what he had seen and heard, and when the statement was reduced to writing, he signed it and swore to it. At the time of the accident Owner was traveling in a train bound for Chicago; Blunt had driven him to the railway station, and was driving the car back to Owner's garage at the time he ran into Pedestrian.

Pedestrian's injuries were serious but during the first few weeks he appeared to be recovering. During this period he was visited by his wife, by his regular attorney, Allen, and on one occasion by Owner. Later his condition grew worse, and when it was apparent that he was about to die, the Assistant District Attorney, Denton, visited him and took a dying declaration from him. Later Blunt was apprehended, charged with negligent homicide of Pedestrian, convicted and sentenced. At Blunt's trial, Warren, Watson, Denton, Vaughn, and Blunt testified. Samuel Scribe, a court reporter, took the testimony verbatim and later transcribed it. While in prison Blunt was fatally wounded in a fight with another prisoner and made a dying declaration to the deputy warden, Kepler. Mrs. Pedestrian later brought action by Charles Cullen, attorney, against Owner for the wrongful death of Pedestrian.

At the trial of this action, the following evidence was offered.

1. Plaintiff called Walter Warren. On direct examination he testified that he saw the automobile which struck Pedestrian when it was about half a block from the crossing where the accident occurred. It was traveling at a high rate of speed, at least 45 miles an hour. He did not see Pedestrian before the accident and did not see the automobile hit him. He heard the crash, saw the car slow up and then pick up speed and turn off at the next corner. He saw Pedestrian sprawled on the grass back of the curb, a couple of yards beyond the crossing, ran to him, and called loudly for help. William Watson got there at almost the same instant and hurried away to call an ambulance. He did not return. Policeman Vaughn came within a couple of minutes. Warren told Vaughn what he had observed and Vaughn made notes of it. Vaughn made him repeat several things, for he, Warren, was much excited and shocked, so much so that he had to go home instead of going to his office after the ambulance came. He helped Vaughn and the ambulance man put Pedestrian into the ambulance. Pedestrian seemed to be unconscious. Some four or five hours later, after he had rested at home and thought over the whole incident carefully, he went to the office of Notary Gore, dictated a true and detailed statement to Gore's stenographer who took it on the typewriter as he dictated; then he signed the statement and swore to it, and it was notarized by Gore. He mailed the statement to Pedestrian's home address, and kept a carbon copy of it. At the trial of Blunt for the negligent homicide of Pedestrian, he testi-

fied just as he has testified here. He used the notarized statement before testifying at that trial to refresh his memory, and did so before coming on the stand this time. Both there and here his memory was completely refreshed. He remembered the scene clearly.

After the direct examination was concluded, the court ordered a recess for the noon hour. During the recess, Warren suffered a fatal heart attack. When this fact was stipulated upon the opening of court for the afternoon session, defendant moved for a mistrial and that the direct examination be stricken. The court denied the motion for a mistrial but granted the motion to strike, and instructed the jury that they should disregard Warren's testimony and treat the case as if he had not testified.

This ruling was in accord with the few pertinent decisions, and represents the generally accepted opinion of the Bar.[1] The defendant had, and could have had, no opportunity to cross-examine, and the lack of opportunity was not due to anything for which he was responsible, or to any voluntary conduct of the witness. No consideration was given to the other circumstances which make the testimony worthy of belief. Warren was a competent, unprivileged witness; he was testifying under oath to relevant, unprivileged matter, confronting the defendant and expecting to be cross-examined by him in the presence of the trier of fact, who could observe every detail of his demeanor which affected his credibility. If the principle upon which this decision is based were to be generally enforced, no evi-

[1] See People v. Cole, 43 N.Y. 508 (1871). I have deemed it superfluous to give citations for the orthodox rules hereinafter discussed. Ample precedents are easily available.

dence of a statement of what a person had perceived could be received over objection by the party against whom it was offered unless he had had opportunity for adequate cross-examination or had lost the opportunity because of his own voluntary conduct or that of the witness. That would eliminate almost every exception to the hearsay rule.

The problem here presented is not usually treated as involving hearsay. It is not separately considered in the American Law Institute Model Code or in the Uniform Rules of Evidence. The evidence does not fall within the definition of hearsay in either, for the statement is made in the process of testifying at the pending trial, and it would be admissible, which must mean usable by the trier of fact when admitted, under Rule 9 of the Model Code and Rule 7 of the Uniform Rules. These rules make all relevant evidence admissible and abolish all privileges, except as otherwise provided in later rules, and no later rule is applicable. The rules tentatively approved by the Advisory Committee of the Supreme Court of Puerto Rico expressly provide for the retention of the evidence when the lack of opportunity of cross-examination is due to no fault of the proponent or the witness or to a sustained claim of privilege.

2. Watson, called as the second witness, testified that he remembered having seen the accident and having telephoned for an ambulance. He also remembered having testified at the Blunt trial after having first talked with Warren and having read Warren's sworn statement. His recollection had been thus refreshed and he had testified to what he had seen and heard as he then remembered it. Before taking the stand at this action by Mrs. Pedestrian

against Owner he had, at plaintiff's request, reread the transcript of his testimony at the Blunt trial and the Warren affidavit, but neither revived his memory so that he could speak from present memory. He was sure that at the time of the Blunt trial he knew what had happened and that the facts were as he then testified and were as stated in the Warren affidavit, so sure in fact that he would be glad to adopt and read to the court and jury as his testimony either the transcript of his former testimony or Warren's affidavit, but he could not from present memory answer any question about what he had perceived at the scene of the accident. Thereupon, plaintiff offered in evidence the Warren affidavit.

The judge sustained defendant's objection. The sworn statement of Warren was not made by Watson. It was not checked and verified by Watson at or about the time of the events and conditions it purported to record, and even if at the time he first read it, he then believed he had a present memory of those matters which needed no reviving, still the danger of his accepting the statement as true merely because it was what Warren and the prosecutor wanted him to remember was too great. It would be going as far as wise caution would allow to permit him to use it as a device for actual refreshment of his recollection. Of course, if Warren had been the witness and had verified the affidavit as a true account of what he had perceived, and his memory had been in precisely the same condition as Watson's memory, the content of the affidavit would have been admissible though the cross-examination would have been equally futile, or, if you will, equally effective.

3. As the next witness, Scribe, the court reporter at the Blunt trial, testified that he had correctly taken in shorthand the entire testimony of Warren including cross-examination. He had with him his shorthand notes and the typewritten transcript which correctly translated those notes into words. It was stipulated by counsel that the transcript was accurate and complete, and defendant agreed that it should be used as an accurate statement of Warren's testimony, if that former testimony was admissible. Thereupon, plaintiff offered the transcript in evidence. On defendant's objection, it was rejected as inadmissible hearsay.

This ruling is supported by universal judicial authority. Why? Warren was unavailable by death. The sanctions under which he had testified were powerful subjective stimuli. He was under oath and confronting a defendant whose liberty was at stake, and expecting to be cross-examined by him. He had no interest in the outcome, and men are usually reluctant to falsify against one who is charged with a serious offense. Warren was not only subject to cross-examination but was cross-examined by a party who had the strongest motive to expose defects in his narration, memory, and perception as well as any lack of sincerity on his part. Had Owner had the opportunity to cross-examine, his interest and motive for doing so could not have been greater. But he had no such opportunity, and that fact is decisive.

To be sure, if Mrs. Pedestrian and Owner had been successors in interest to the respective parties in the earlier trial, Warren's former testimony would have been admissible. The only rational explanation for this qualification of this exclusionary rule is that the successors have the same interest and motives to present the evidence and to cross-examine as their respective predecessors, but the usual judicial opinion makes no reference to this highly pertinent factor; it talks only of the applicability of the *res adjudicata* doctrine—a doctrine which has no relation whatever to the reliability of the evidence upon which the pertinent binding decision is based.

Moreover, even if Warren had been present and subject to cross-examination but had shown that he could not speak from present memory, his former testimony would have been inadmissible; but the content of his properly verified statement in writing, made before Notary Gore, whether sworn to or not, would have been receivable as a record of his past recollection and a substitute for his present recollection. If, however, he had testified from present memory, neither his former testimony nor his affidavit would have been receivable as evidence of the truth of their respective contents, although they might have been admissible to impeach him. The verification made by him in his direct examination, which had been stricken, was, of course, no longer in the record. Whatever explanation, based on historical accident, may be advanced to explain the original judicial acceptance of these curious doctrines, something more is required to justify their application in current litigation.

4. Plaintiff before releasing Scribe as a witness had him identify a typed transcript of the testimony given by Watson at the Blunt trial and, after stipulations as to its accuracy were entered of record, offered it in evidence. The

court ruled it inadmissible for the same reasons upon which the exclusion of Warren's former testimony was based.

5. Policeman Vaughn was plaintiff's next witness. He testified that he had heard Warren's testimony, that on the occasion in question he heard a call for help and hurriedly answered it. He reached the scene within a minute or two and found Warren bending over Pedestrian who was lying on the grass a few yards from the crossing between the sidewalk and the curb. Warren said that someone had gone to telephone for an ambulance; he, Vaughn, asked Warren how the accident happened. Warren was nervous and excited and talked so rapidly that he had to be told to take it easy and talk more slowly so that Vaughn could make full notes, that he took such notes, had them with him, and could by consulting them tell what Warren had said. When he was asked to do so, defendant objected. The objection was overruled. Vaughn's answer was substantially a repetition of the description of the accident in the testimony given by Warren as the first witness in the trial, testimony which the court had stricken.

The court's ruling admitting evidence of Warren's statement under an exception to the hearsay rule was in accord with all modern judicial opinions. It was admissible under Thayer's theory that the statement was substantially contemporaneous with the event and made on the scene where there were still traces of the event visible to the witness, or under Wigmore's theory that it was made while the speaker was under a stress of nervous excitement caused by the exciting event which the statement describes or explains. Under Thayer's theory the witness who reports the statement is subject to cross-examination concerning the circumstances under which it was made and the conditions at the scene, and the trier need not rely upon the uncorroborated statement alone. Under Wigmore's theory the statement is unreflective or spontaneous; to use the language of some courts, it is the event rather than the declarant that speaks. The declarant had no time, no opportunity, to contrive. This can mean only that the circumstances of the utterance serve in some way as a substitute for the oath. They affect only sincerity. Memory is not involved. But use of language is of some importance and accuracy of perception is vital. If we may believe the psychologists, both observation and narration in circumstances of excitement are less than normally accurate, and the need for cross-examination is greater.

If Warren had been the witness testifying concerning the accident, he too would have been permitted to repeat what he had told Vaughn and it would have been usable to prove the truth of the matter asserted in it. But he would not have been allowed to make a like use of his statement to Gore, which was made with care and under oath. His unsworn statement is preferred to his sworn statement. The substitute for the oath is a more effective guaranty of sincerity than the oath itself. A man's unreflective statement, be he ever so interested in the matter stated, is more likely to represent what he actually believes, than his later statement deliberately made under oath. Furthermore, if the sworn statement had been made by Warren while testifying in a previous trial of the same case under oath subject and actually subjected to cross-examination by this defendant, it would have been equally inadmissible. This surely approaches a puzzling paradox. A reasonably adequate guaranty of sincerity, in a situation where memory is not involved but correct interpretation of language is of some importance and accuracy of perception is very material, is to be preferred to both the safeguards normally required to assure reliability—oath and cross-examination.

6. Notary Gore was called and testified as to the time and circumstances in which Warren's affidavit was made and identified the writing. Thereupon plaintiff offered again the transcripts of Warren's and Watson's testimony and offered the affidavit, pointing out that all three were consistent in all material statements and thus verified each other. The court rejected the offer.

7. Denton, the assistant district attorney, when called, produced a writing, all of which except the signature he testified was written by him at the dictation of Pedestrian. The signature was that of Pedestrian made after he, Denton, had correctly read to him what was written. Before starting to dictate, Pedestrian had said that he had been told by his physician that he had only a very short time to live, knew he was dying, and wanted Denton to know how careless the driver of the automobile had been so that the prosecutor's office could take appropriate action. The physician, who was present, confirmed Pedestrian's statement as to Pedestrian's hopeless condition. The writing, Denton testified, had been received in evidence at the homicide trial of Blunt and had been withdrawn with the consent of the court for use at this trial. Plaintiff offered the writing in evidence. Defendant's objection was sustained.

There is no question that the dying declaration had been properly received in the criminal case. In the absence of statute, there is also no doubt that it was properly rejected in this civil action and would have been everywhere rejected, except only in Kansas, even though the issue had to do with precisely the same matters, namely, the events or conditions which immediately caused the death.

The orthodox explanation for its reception in homicide prosecutions is that the realization of speedily impending death furnishes a sanction as powerful as the oath and the prospect of cross-examination. The early assumption was that the declarant had a firm belief in a hereafter where punishment was inflicted for sin; no one would go to meet his Maker with a lie on his lips. The later decisions require no such belief; the awfulness of the situation is said to provide a sufficient sanction, and even contemporaneous conduct manifesting a total lack of awe, to say nothing of reverence, operates only to decrease the value of the statement. It is needless to point out that there is no substitute for cross-examination, and that the required state of mind of the declarant makes clarity of memory and accuracy of expression at least doubtful. Still, if the evidence is of enough value to be used against a person where his liberty or even his life depends upon the verdict, it should be of no less value where it can injure only his interest in property. If it be said, as a few courts declare, that its admissibility is confined to homicide prosecutions and there justified only because of the high importance of bringing manslayers to justice, it may be asked whether the policy of protecting an accused from serious punishment is not as imperative as that of saving him from pecuniary harm. If untrustworthy evidence is sufficient to jeopardize a man's life or liberty, what policy can make it insufficient to subject him to the risk of pecuniary liability?

8. Plaintiff next called Kepler, who identified a writing signed by Blunt and who testified that it correctly recorded a statement made a few hours before Blunt's death, after the prison surgeon in Kepler's presence had told Blunt that he was fatally wounded and had but a short time to live. The first sentence of the writing was: "I believe that I am about to die and make this statement with no hope of recovery." After stating the facts as to the fight in which he was wounded, it recited his desire to purge his soul of the sin of having lied at his trial, that in fact he was driving faster than the speed limit; he was going about forty-five in a 25-mile zone, and he was pretty drunk. He was sorry that the expenses of the trial had used up all his money so that he could not leave anything to pay Mrs. Pedestrian for the wrong he had done to her. When plaintiff offered this writing, it was, upon defendant's objection, rejected as hearsay.

This deathbed confession insofar as it concerned the criminal trial would not be admissible in any action, civil or criminal, except in Kansas. The matter concerning the encounter causing Blunt's death would be admissible in a criminal prosecution for his homicide, but not elsewhere. Obviously all the statements therein were made under exactly the same sanctions, and those concerning the previous perjury had a greater disserving quality than the others. Blunt's statement shows he had no thought of having to answer to any charge of civil or criminal liability for the wrongs confessed. If he had, while solvent and expecting to recover, made a statement conceding civil liability to Mrs. Pedestrian but denying criminal responsibility, evidence of the statement would be admissible; but if the concession was of criminal liability without civil liability, it would have been inadmissible. The theory is that no man will concede the existence of a fact which he realizes to be contrary to his pecuniary interest in the sense that it creates a valid claim for money against him or destroys an existing claim or an apparent proprietary interest, unless he believes that fact does exist. The realization of its disserving effect takes the place of the oath. This sounds sensible enough, but the application of the doctrine, particularly by the English courts, passes understanding. An entry in a man's private book reciting a loan to X and payment of interest thereon or part payment of the principal is received as evidence that the money in question was transferred to X as a loan upon the issue whether it was a loan or a gift. An oral or written statement of a person in possession of a parcel of realty that he has paid a specified amount to X as rent for a specified period is admissible wherever relevant in an action between strangers as tending to prove the truth of the statement on the theory that possession of realty raises a presumption of ownership and payment of rent is a concession of lack of ownership and therefore against proprietary interest. Yet these same courts hold inadmissible statements conceding the commission of a criminal act which the declarant did realize, or must have realized, subjected him to the most severe penalties. While the American courts do not go to such fantastic extremes in dealing with statements involving pecuniary or proprietary interests, almost all of them accept the English view as to declarations against penal interest. No court has yet given a respectable reason for the distinction, least of all the House of Lords in the opinions which established it.

9. Plaintiff next offered in evidence a transcript of the testimony of Blunt at his trial for homicide, and particularly, that portion of his cross-examination in which Blunt stated that on his way from the railway station to Owner's garage, he had stopped at Guber's place and taken about four drinks of Scotch straight, in about twenty minutes; this was about ten minutes before the accident.

Defendant conceded the correctness of the transcript but objected to the evidence as hearsay. The objection was sustained for the same reasons as were applied in rejecting the transcripts of Warren's and Watson's testimony. When proponent insisted that the declaration was against Blunt's interest, the court ruled it was against Blunt's penal interest but not against his pecuniary interest, and not admissible.

10. Frederick Foster testified for plaintiff that he had been a friend of Blunt, that on the day of the accident he met Blunt at the railway station, and that Blunt invited him to ride with him. When plaintiff asked him what conversation he had had with Blunt, and defendant's objection was tentatively sustained, plaintiff offered to prove that Foster would testify that Blunt had said that he was going to take the car to Owner's garage, that he was to have the

afternoon off, was going to stop at Guber's and have a few shots of Scotch to get him in the right mood for a holiday, and that he would buy drinks also for Foster. Foster rode with Blunt to Guber's but declined his invitation to go in and drink. Defendant's objection to the offer was overruled, and Foster testified accordingly.

The judge's ruling was supported by the great weight of current authority. This is a declaration of a presently existing state of mind made without circumstances of suspicion. Because such a statement is frequently made while the declarant is doing a relevant act, as in this case driving the car to the garage, the opinions are clouded by talk of *res gestae*, but the more recent decisions squarely recognize a separate exception to the hearsay rule, covering declarations of a presently existing subjective condition.

The result of the last two rulings applying accepted doctrine is to use a declaration of intent with no apparent realization of any disserving aspect of the declaration, as evidence that Blunt did the act, after rejecting Blunt's statement that he had done the act, made under oath in open court when he must have realized that it was highly prejudicial.

11. Plaintiff then offered a certified copy of the judgment roll in the Blunt case, consisting of the indictment, record of the arraignment and plea, the verdict and sentence. On objection, it was rejected. The indictment was pure hearsay if offered to prove Blunt's guilt; the verdict likewise was hearsay opinion and was based on testimony which when given was not subject to cross-examination by this defendant; and the judgment was no better. By the

majority view it would not have been received even in a civil action against Blunt for the injury and death of Pedestrian, and no court would admit it against any stranger to the criminal action. A layman might think that the result of a proceeding in which the truth of the disputed proposition had been established beyond reasonable doubt was at least worth considering in any inquiry concerning the matter in dispute. But laymen do not understand our adversary system of litigation.

12. Finally plaintiff took the stand, and testified that after her husband's funeral, the defendant called upon her, and talked with her about the accident. When asked what he had said concerning Blunt's conduct, defendant objected and offered to prove that at the time of the accident he was on a train bound for Chicago, and that he first learned about it after he returned some five or six days later. The objection was overruled on the ground that any relevant statement by him was receivable against him as an admission whether or not it was based on his own observation. Plaintiff then answered that defendant said he was very sorry about the whole matter, that Blunt was to blame for he was drunk at the time, and that he would be punished, that he, Owner, had talked with Attorney Allen and would see him again.

When plaintiff rested the defendant moved for a directed verdict. He conceded that Blunt was his servant acting in the scope of his employment and had driven the car into contact with Pedestrian, that Pedestrian died as a result of the injuries thus inflicted, and that the plaintiff was his widow. The court ruled that the testimony of Vaughn, of

Foster, and of plaintiff was sufficient to justify a verdict for plaintiff, and denied the motion.

Defendant took the stand and testified that about a week or ten days after the accident he had visited Pedestrian at the hospital and found him cheerful though he had one arm and one leg in a cast, and that he had a conversation with him about the accident. When he was asked to state the conversation, objection was interposed by plaintiff that the witness was an interested survivor and incompetent under the so-called dead man statute to testify to any conduct of decedent and particularly to any conversation with him. Defendant thereupon offered to prove that Pedestrian told him that he thought Blunt should be prosecuted for driving so as to endanger life; that he had told his wife how the accident happened and asked her to send his attorney, Allen, to see him; that Allen had called, and he, Pedestrian, had told Allen the whole story and Allen had asked him a lot of questions, some of them like a lawyer on cross-examination; that Allen said he would see Owner and try to get a good settlement; that it was no open-and-shut case; and that the account of the accident in the newspaper wasn't so good. The court ruled that even if this could be regarded as a vicarious admission by a predecessor in interest of the plaintiff, still the statute was too obviously applicable for debate and sustained the objection. Similar statutes exist in the great majority of our states; their provisions vary greatly, but none of them are more sweeping or arbitrary than those in force in New York, and none have required so many interpretative decisions. All are based upon the delusion that perjury can be prevented by making interested persons incompetent or by excluding certain classes of testimony. They persist in spite of experience which demonstrates that they defeat the honest litigant and rarely, if ever, prevent the dishonest from introducing the desired evidence: if the dishonest party is prevented from committing perjury, he is not prevented from suborning it. If the statutes protect the estates of the dead from some false claims, they damage the estates of the living to a much greater extent. And frequently their application prevents proof of a valid claim by the representative of decedent's estate.

The Commonwealth Fund Committee, the American Law Institute, the American Bar Association, and the Uniform Law Commissioners, as well as the leading commentators, have urged the abolition of this last remnant of disqualification of witnesses on account of interest. But they have had very little influence upon the legislatures, perhaps because no intelligent effort has been made to present the pertinent considerations to the legislatures in a practical manner.

Defendant proceeded to testify that when he had called upon Mrs. Pedestrian, she said that she had asked Attorney Allen to visit her husband at the hospital and had talked with Allen both before and after her husband's death, that she read the newspaper account of the accident on the day after it occurred but that she knew nothing about the facts except what her husband had told her.

Defendant next called plaintiff as his witness. She testified that she had visited her husband often at the hospital and had had long conversations with him, that she also had had conversations with Attorney Allen both before and after her husband's death. Her present attorney, Mr. Cullen, was never consulted by her husband, so far as she knew. She retained him on the advice of some of her relatives after Allen had been unable to get a settlement with defendant.

When asked what her husband had told her, if anything, about his conduct at the moment when, and a few moments before, he stepped off the curb, she claimed a privilege not to answer because the question called for a privileged communication between husband and wife. The judge sustained the privilege. This privilege in some form is said by Wigmore and assumed by many American courts to be a common-law privilege, and is embodied in numerous statutes. Though it is the privilege of the communicating spouse, it is not terminated by his death, and may be claimed by his successor in interest. It is immaterial that, if true, it would destroy a claim sought to be enforced by the successor.

Defendant offered to prove that the newspaper account of the accident stated that this was another case of the careless pedestrian, and that the plaintiff as witness would testify that in the conversation with her husband, he had told her that he stepped off the curb without looking while his attention was distracted. He was looking at a memorandum of an address of a person he was going to call on. The judge refused the offer.

Defendant then asked plaintiff if she had tried to retain Mr. Allen as her attorney in this action, and whether he had refused the retainer. Over objection, the court required her to answer, and she said, "Yes." When asked why he had refused, the court upheld an objection on the ground that it called for a privileged communication between attorney and client. There is little, if any, doubt of the correctness of this ruling. Although the privilege is phrased in terms of confidential communications of client to attorney, it applies also to those from attorney to client, and negotiations for retainer are included in the privilege.

Defendant finally called Attorney Allen who testified that he had been retained by Pedestrian and had attempted to negotiate a settlement with defendant, both before and after Pedestrian's death. Plaintiff had sought to retain him to bring action for her husband's wrongful death but he had refused. When asked to state the reasons for his refusal, he answered that he could not do so without divulging confidential communications between himself and Pedestrian when he was Pedestrian's attorney and conversations between himself and plaintiff during negotiations by her for the retainer; he therefore claimed privilege on behalf of both. The plaintiff interposed a like claim. Defendant requested the court to compel both this witness and plaintiff to answer to the court in private, asserting that these answers would show plaintiff's fraud in bringing this action, for Allen's statements to her would be to the effect that she had no case on account of Pedestrian's contributory negligence, and though defendant might not be able to dig up admissible evidence of it, he, Allen, could not conscientiously take the case. With this basis, he might then ask the court to question Attorney Cullen whether plaintiff had disclosed to him what her husband had told her. The court ruled that the mere fact of Allen's refusal of the retainer, the bringing of action by Cullen, and the claim of privilege were not sufficient to raise even a suspicion of fraud; and some evidence of fraud outside the communication was requisite, probably at least enough to justify a finding, before revelation of the communication to the judge could be compelled.

These proceedings took place before a court erected by society for the purpose of resolving by rational process disputes between litigants. The issues involved were simple: (1) Blunt's conduct, (2) Blunt's condition, and (3) Pedestrian's conduct at the time and place when Owner's car collided with Pedestrian. Let me summarize the rulings with a view to the value of the offered evidence as tending to persuade a trier of reasonable intelligence to find what actually happened.

Some eight items of evidence were offered. Four of them had as their source two eyewitnesses who had, so far as was shown, no possible motive to falsify, and both of whom had on at least one occasion been subjected to cross-examination under oath. The source of two of the other items was the actor participant in the event in question and of the remaining two, the participant victim.

As to Blunt's conduct:

1. The jury were forbidden to consider the direct testimony of eyewitness Warren—statements made by him under oath in their presence and in the presence of defendant Owner while expecting to be cross-examined by him.

2. They were prevented from hearing: sworn statements by this same disinterested witness, made some four or five

hours after the occasion, while he was calm and able to be careful of his use of language, and while his recollection was clear and firm.

3. Statements made by him while testifying at the trial of a prior criminal action under oath, confronting the person charged with the offense and cross-examined by him;

4. Sworn statements made by Watson, another eyewitness, made while testifying at the same criminal action, who swore before the present judge and jury that these statements were true to his knowledge at the time he made them;

5. Statements made by Blunt himself when he was on his deathbed and realized that he was about to die;

6. Statements made by Pedestrian, the victim of the accident, an eyewitness, within a few weeks after the event, when he was on his deathbed and realized that he was about to die;

7. Statements made by Pedestrian to his wife, as to the accuracy of which there was no question;

8. Verdict and judgment of guilt of Blunt which necessarily included a finding of the disputed proposition of fact in accord with the offered testimony.

The fact that each of these items was entirely consistent with and corroborated by each of the others was ineffective to make any one of them admissible.

On the other hand, the tribunal heard and properly considered:

(1) An unsworn statement made by Warren to Vaughn when Warren was laboring under the stress of shock and excitement;

(2) An unsworn statement by Owner who had no knowledge concerning the facts.

Concerning Blunt's condition at the time of the event, the tribunal was permitted to hear and consider, (1) Blunt's unsworn statement of intent to take several drinks of whiskey, but (2) not his statement made under oath as a part of his testimony at the criminal trial that he had taken those several drinks. It was permitted to hear and consider (1) the statement of Owner, who could not have observed Blunt for several days after the event, that Blunt was drunk, but (2) not Blunt's own dying declaration.

As to Pedestrian's conduct it was not permitted to hear Pedestrian's own statement—Pedestrian, the one person with peculiar knowledge of the facts.

In short, of all available evidence from eyewitnesses, only those hearsay statements of Warren which were made under the weakest substitute for the usual sanctions were admissible. The most reliable and most persuasive items were inadmissible.

Why should laymen tolerate a system of proof in litigation which in application is so surcharged with irrational inconsistencies? The answer is clear. To the layman the subject of evidence, like that of pleading, is a dark mystery. Only a small percentage of the public ever have occasion to feel or even to observe the impact of the rules in operation.

Then why should judges and lawyers, members of the ancient and honorable profession which is charged with the duty of adjusting between members of society disputes involving their property, their liberty, and their lives be content with rules which in application so often shock common sense?

Is it because in fact these rules only occasionally work great harm in practice? And is it true that the harm is avoided for these reasons?

1. A large part of the Bar has no real acquaintance with them. As Professor Bowie said when working with a committee of the Maryland Bar in drafting rules of pleading: "The rules of common law pleading have been repealed in Maryland by the ignorance of the Bar." And Judge Learned Hand has declared that the American Law Institute made a great mistake in publishing a Model Code of Evidence, for it caused lawyers and judges to revive rules which were practically dead or at least buried in oblivion.

2. When a case of importance is being tried by counsel of repute who desire a decision on the merits, they do not insist upon observance of the rules, except only where the enforcement of an exclusionary rule would be practically decisive.

3. The courts of last resort find the rules a very present help in time of trouble. If the verdict and judgment represent what they believe to be a sound result, they find alleged errors in the admission or exclusion of evidence to have been nonprejudicial. If they feel impelled to disapprove the result, violation of a rule of evidence constitutes reversible error.

All this may be akin to professional treason. Perhaps no opinion of a professor of law should be taken too seriously by men who have to deal with the facts of life in the courtroom. It may also be possible, though I am most reluctant to concede it, that preachments such as this—preachments which I have been making for lo these many years—properly go unheeded for the same reason that the best conversational efforts of the most charming dinner guest of his hostess failed to move Sir Frederick Pollock to conversation. When chided by his hostess, he replied, "Well really, you know, she didn't say anything that seemed to call for an answer."

# INDEX

www.ingramcontent.com/pod-product-compliance
Ingram Content Group UK Ltd.
Pitfield, Milton Keynes, MK11 3LW, UK
UKHW020211290926
15470UKWH00001B/121

9 780837 185170